Stage Presence
from Head to Toe

A Manual for Musicians

Karen A. Hagberg

The Scarecrow Press, Inc.
Lanham, Maryland, and Oxford
2003

SCARECROW PRESS, INC.

Published in the United States of America
by Scarecrow Press, Inc.
A Member of the Rowman & Littlefield Publishing Group
4501 Forbes Boulevard, Suite 200, Lanham, Maryland 20706
www.scarecrowpress.com

PO Box 317
Oxford
OX2 9RU, UK

British Library Cataloguing in Publication Information Available

Library of Congress Cataloging-in-Publication Data

Hagberg, Karen A., 1943–
  Stage presence from head to toe : a manual for musicians / Karen A.
Hagberg.
    p. cm.
  Includes bibliographical references (p. 103) and index.
  ISBN 0-8108-4777-9 (pbk. : alk. paper)
  1. Music—Performance. 2. Concerts—Handbooks, manuals, etc. 3.
Concert etiquette. 4. Self-confidence. I. Title.
ML3795.H13 2003
781.4'3—dc21
                            2003004846

Printed in the United States of America

This book is dedicated to the survival of
live, acoustic music in the twenty-first century.

Contents

Contents

Illustrations

Checklists

Acknowledgments

This book is the result of my happy association with the following people, who contributed to various aspects of its writing.

These personnel staff members in the following orchestras responded to my questionnaire about their onstage guidelines: Russell Williamson (Atlanta Symphony); Anne MacQuarrie (Chicago Symphony Orchestra); Nicholas Hansinger (Detroit Symphony Orchestra); Laura Hutchason Hearn (Kennedy Center Opera House Orchestra); Ted Hutman (Los Angeles Philharmonic Orchestra); Linda Uhkefer (Milwaukee Symphony Orchestra); Heather Larson (Minnesota Orchestra); Everett Zlatoff-Mirsky (Lyric Opera of Chicago Orchestra); Vurl Bland (Nashville Symphony); Harold Steiman (Pittsburgh Symphony Orchestra); Drew Cady (San Diego Symphony); and Gregory Quick (Syracuse Symphony Orchestra).

The following musicians posed for photographs used as reference for the illustrations: David Angus (horn), Sheri Blake (piano), Lisa Cash (piano), Justin Gardner (piano), Laura Griffiths (oboe), Larissa Hoffend (piano), Kathleen Murphy Kemp (cello), Lisa McCollum (voice), Teri Paradero (piano), and Tigran Vardanian (violin).

I am indebted to these musicians, friends, and family for their individual contributions: R. J. Alcala, a wonderful musician, talented editor, and long-standing friend, who painstakingly thought about every word I wrote, replaced many with better ones, and at whose suggestion I included the chapter on teaching stage presence; Carlene Ames, my muse, for her faith in me and in the project; David Angus, horn player in the Rochester Philharmonic Orchestra and president of the International Conference of Symphony and Orchestra Musicians, for providing invaluable contact information and advice; John Cammarasano, graphic artist, who produced the illustrations; Annette Dragon, photographer and friend, for helping at the last minute with her state-of-the-art equipment; Richard Elliott, Tabernacle organist for the Mormon Tabernacle Choir, for sharing the stage deportment guidelines he developed for his own students; Louise Goldberg, Ph.D., my friend and colleague, for professional advice, good ideas, and invaluable contacts; Ceil Goldman, my dear friend and editor, who has guided and encouraged this project since it was just an idea; my mother, Elsie Hagberg, who applied the no-nonsense advice of her high school English teacher; Douglas Humpherys, associate professor of piano at the Eastman School of Music, for evaluating the chapter on competitions and auditions; Dr. Haruko Kataoka, founder of the Suzuki Piano Basics Method, who taught me the importance of stage presence from the point of view of both the performer and the audience; Barry Lane, my brother-in-law's brother-in law, owner of the consulting firm Discover Writing, who advised me on the ins and outs of the publishing world; Ralph Locke, chair of the Department of Musicology at the Eastman School of Music, for good advice early in the project; Russell Miller, assistant professor of vocal coaching and repertoire at the Eastman School of Music, for lending a critical eye to the final manuscript and providing useful suggestions; Sue Rarus, director of information services at the National Association for Music Education (MENC), for supplying me with statistical data; Gail Seneca, more family than friend, whose meteoric rise in the business world after "dressing for success" was, I realize, a major inspiration for this book; Allison Sharma, my niece, who heard an interview by Leonard Slatkin on the radio and alerted me to its contents; Jeff Tyzik, composer, arranger, and conductor, who offered valuable suggestions for the chapters on orchestras and conductors; Lawrence Wechsler, horn player in the Metropolitan Opera Orchestra, who enlightened me on matters specific to the pit orchestra; my sister Elsa Worth, who provided invaluable editing and many good suggestions; and finally to my partner, Dorothy Drake, who saw purses hanging on the backs of the violinists' chairs and said, "Why doesn't anyone tell them not to do that?"

—KH

Introduction

This book focuses on the performance of classical music, but the basic principles are the same for all kinds of music. Musicians need to make their audiences receptive and to give them a lasting, positive impression. Just as classical training lays a foundation for the performance of other kinds of music, the basics of stage presence outlined here may be adapted to all kinds of performances, by all kinds of musicians.

Stage presence is an aspect of music education that carries over to many other areas of life. Good stage presence is invaluable for job interviews, verbal presentations, and social situations of all kinds.

For the musician, good stage presence helps to build and keep audiences. This is so important, for without the audience, there can be no performances. Too many fine performers and ensembles do not rise to their deserved level of success because they lack the ability to relate to their audience appropriately and effectively. I have written this book as a manual and guide for those musicians who need help looking more comfortable, confident, and appropriate on stage and for teachers who want to impart stage presence skills to their students. This book summarizes the accepted guidelines as they have come down to us in the twenty-first century after over two hundred years of public musical performances.

It should be mentioned that, from the rise of public performance in the late eighteenth century, some very successful and famous musicians have broken the conventional "rules" of stage presence by wearing attention-getting attire and engaging in unconventional behavior on stage. Franz Liszt was an early, and notorious, example. His fame (like that of Elvis Presley and Liberace more recently) was the result of becoming a heart-throb and a matinee idol as much as being a musician.

No one should argue that these great performers had poor stage presence. On the contrary, they each had an uncanny ability to connect with
their audience. Consider, however, that no performer can make an impression in this way unless there are standards from which to deviate.
This book outlines the standards as they have come down to us in the
twenty-first century.

Chapter 1

Stage Presence

The piece of music is worked out by the composer, but it is the performance which we enjoy. Thus the active and emotional principle in music occurs in the act of reproduction, which draws the electric spark from a mysterious source and directs it toward the heart of the listener.

—Eduard Hanslick (1825–1904), music critic

Music does not exist until it is performed.

—Benjamin Britten (1913–1976), composer

Think about the best concert you have ever attended—a concert that thrilled you—that left you feeling you had just experienced something wonderful and out of the ordinary—a concert at which you felt deeply touched by the music. Truly exceptional musical performances produce this kind of experience.

On the other hand, many concerts seem to be played well enough, but just have no spark. You may leave the concert hall remembering only such things as the sheet music hanging precariously off the edge of the music stand or the violinist in the third row who wore white socks. These seemingly little distractions have the power to pull the audience away from the music, so that no matter how well the musicians are playing, the audience will have a hard time being moved by the performance.

Impeccable stage presence, always a component of the best performances, is a topic musicians too often disregard. This is shortsighted, because good stage presence has far more impact on the audience than performers sometimes consider or realize, and it can be the key element

1

in the making or breaking of a concert, no matter how well the musicians play.

What exactly is stage presence, and why is it important for musicians?

STAGE PRESENCE DEFINED

Stage presence is the visual aspect of a live musical performance: everything from a performer's walk, bow, facial expression, and dress, to an ensemble's portrayal of a single, unified entity; from the condition of chairs, music stands, and piano, to the mechanics of smooth stage management. Performers can greatly enhance their image, and their audience's total experience, by paying attention to the details of stage presence.

Good stage presence, like good editing in films or books, goes largely unnoticed. Though it does not announce itself, it allows the audience to be in a positive, receptive mood before the concert, and allows listeners to concentrate on the music throughout the performance without distractions. Performers with good stage presence project a positive image: they know what they are doing and have meticulously attended to every detail of their work.

Poor stage presence is painfully obvious. We in the audience feel nervous when we watch a soloist who is nervous. An awkward performer makes us feel awkward, too. And we can become very distracted by an ensemble whose members are distracted. The shoulder strap that keeps slipping down the violinist's arm, the hair that constantly falls into the pianist's face, or the short pant legs that reveal bare skin over the cellist's socks all draw attention away from the music.

There are innumerable little things involving performers' nervous habits and inappropriate onstage behavior that may constitute poor stage presence as well. A wise performer anticipates and, as much as possible, eliminates all potential distractions.

THE PHILOSOPHICAL BASIS: RESPECT

The first requisite in a musician is, that he should respect, acknowledge, and do homage to what is great and sublime in his art, instead of trying to extinguish the great lights, so that his own small one may shine a little more brightly.

—Felix Mendelssohn (1809–1847), composer, conductor, pianist

Stage presence is not simply a long list of rules of behavior. No rulebook exists that prescribes the proper way to perform in all settings at all times. Good stage presence, like music itself, is an art, a clear expression of the disciplined musician's respect for the music, for the audience, for other musicians, and for himself or herself.

Respect for the Music

As the performer, you should do everything you can to provide the audience with direct access to the music, with as few distractions as possible. When you respect the music you readily defer to the composer and do nothing that could take the spotlight away from the work being played. You are also prepared to perform by having adequately practiced so that your performance is as good as it can be. Do not let the performance look or sound like a rehearsal.

Respect for the Audience

Respecting the audience means appreciating the people who took the time and trouble to come and listen. After all, without them there would be no performance. When you are appreciative of your audience, you will sincerely want to do your best for them, and this will be reflected in your facial expressions and body language. Audiences, like guests, will feel welcome if you greet them with genuine friendliness and respect.

Respect for Other Musicians

Never do anything to bring attention to yourself or take attention away from the group. When musicians play together, competition among them can seriously detract from the performance. Respecting your fellow musicians means that you do not try to upstage them in any way; for example, the accompanist should dress more conservatively than the soloist, the members of the string section should remain still and attentive during the flute solo, and every member of an ensemble should keep an eye on the conductor at all times. All musicians should be present throughout the performance of a work and not leave the stage during long rests or before the applause is finished. The physical space of those around you should not be violated with demonstrative or sudden body movements. Ensemble bows need to be rehearsed, giving all members appropriate and gracious acknowledgment.

Respect for Yourself

When you respect yourself as a musician, you take your work seriously, and you want your audience to take you seriously as well. You have practiced long hours and have gone to the trouble to arrange for a performance.

After all of this, you do not want to look awkward or foolish onstage, nor do you want inadvertently to put off your audience in any way. Attending to the most minute details of your stage presence indicates a respect for both yourself and your work that will enhance your image in the eyes of your audience and the general public.

STAGE PRESENCE AND STAGE FRIGHT

The determination to give pleasure does more to nullify stage fright than any device known.

—George Hotchkiss Street (twentieth century), vocal coach, professor

Unfortunately, many fine musicians are not able to perform successfully in front of an audience because of stage fright. Every performer must cope with feelings of anxiety before a concert because it takes courage to get up in front of an audience and do *anything*, much less a task as complex as playing a musical instrument or singing. All successful performers must find ways to deal with this inevitable anxiety.

Despite the hazards of stage fright, the adrenaline produced by preconcert excitement can actually help performers do their best. We humans accomplish the most when our adrenaline is pumping. This is the reason athletes almost always break records in competitions and not during practice sessions. Musicians who have learned to use this heightened state to their advantage find that adrenaline can spur them on to do their best rather than cause them to fall apart.

Knowing Helps

While much has been written about stage fright as a phobia that in some cases might need medical attention, very little has been said about the relationship between stage fright and stage presence. Good stage presence can actually help relieve much of the anxiety associated with stage fright.

In any situation, stress is reduced when you know what is expected of you and how to go about doing things correctly. In a social context, for example, you are much more at ease if you know how to make introductions properly, converse with strangers, or even which fork to use at the dinner table. Without knowing such basics of etiquette, you may feel insecure and awkward. If you were continually to make one etiquette faux pas after another, your insecurity could turn into full-blown anxiety. This kind of snowballing embarrassment can cause some people to become so anxious that they avoid social situations.

Musicians in performance are no different. If unsure how to walk onto a stage, how to bow, where to stand, how to face the audience, how to hold the instrument, how to dress, and so on, a musician can also become anxious, sometimes to the point of not being able to perform at all. Knowing the basic rules, and then following them, gives the musician a sense of self-confidence and self-control. Just as most people need to practice shaking hands with strangers while looking into their eyes and smiling as they introduce themselves, musicians, too, must practice walking on stage, bowing, and then properly getting ready to play. Though more natural to some people than others, these are all acquired skills without which musicians would be much less able to handle stage fright. Performers can increase their sense of self-confidence and self-control, overcome their nervousness, and use the pressure of performance to their advantage on stage by studying and practicing the principles of good stage presence.

Knowing you look your best and are acting appropriately on stage takes away debilitating self-consciousness and allows you to think about the music and about bringing pleasure to the audience. Stage fright is exaggerated when your attention is focused solely on yourself. Learning to become centered on the music itself and on the performance at hand is essential for players who want to minimize stage fright.

PAYING ATTENTION TO STAGE PRESENCE IS IMPORTANT FOR MUSICIANS

Good stage presence complements and enhances a musical performance, while poor stage presence not only diminishes a performance but can also ruin it entirely. Good stage presence reflects a musician's respect for the music, the audience, for other musicians, and for himself or herself. Practicing good stage presence can allow a musician to use the rush of adrenaline before a performance to his or her advantage, effectively diminishing stage fright. Compared with the complexities and demands of learning to perform a musical work, stage presence may seem to be unimportant, but it is a vital element of the performance that no musician can afford to overlook.

Chapter 2

The Soloist

The pianist's physical impression is enormously important, more important than I ever supposed as a beginner. . . . I didn't realize how important [it] was until the first time I saw myself on television. Before that, if anyone commented on my appearance I thought, "Here I'm trying to perform great music, and they're talking about banalities." I made all sorts of bad movements; I threw my arms wildly about. When I finally saw how I looked, however, I realized that I was distracting the audience from the music.

—Alfred Brendel (b. 1931), pianist

Learning the music and expressing it in your own unique way is, of course, your primary task as a performer. It is good to realize, however, that visual aspects of your presentation either help or hinder the audience's ability to be drawn into your music. Are you confident and enthusiastic about performing? Did you take the time to look your best? Have you organized your stage management so that it runs smoothly and does not take up unnecessary time? Have you done everything possible to eliminate repetitious, possibly annoying, body or facial movements? Performers who pay attention to these things look comfortable onstage and, in turn, put the audience at ease and ready to listen. You owe it to yourself, after all your long hours of practice, to present your music in the best context.

HOW TO DRESS FOR THE CONCERT STAGE

Dressing for Style

We all have our individual styles of dress in everyday life, and some of us are more fashion conscious than others. It is important to realize, however, that a musical performance is not a fashion show, and that care must be taken to choose appropriate dress for a concert.

The level of formality of your clothing, for example, may vary depending on the time of day of the performance (generally, less formal for afternoons than evenings), the time of year (less formal in the summertime than during other seasons), or the venue (less formal in a room than in a concert hall), but every performance, whether before an audience or judges, deserves a dressed up appearance. If you wear everyday clothes you risk having your performance look like a rehearsal or a practice session. Dressing up also indicates that you take yourself seriously, and suggests that the audience should do so as well.

In addition to the level of formality in dress, musicians need to be sensitive to how flamboyant or revealing their clothing might be. Those who dress in provocative clothing in their everyday lives should recognize that such styles may be inappropriate while performing simply because they compete with the music for the audience's attention. Some young professional performers are encouraged by their agents to adopt unusual or provocative modes of dress so that audiences will remember them (the young man with the big muscles or the red socks; the young woman with the stunning cleavage or the short skirt); and some achieve notoriety by discarding traditional conventions of concert attire altogether. Revealing and unconventional clothing, however, distracts an audience. For example, it is not uncommon lately to see musicians performing with bare arms—but as the conductor Leonard Slatkin pointed out in an interview in the *London Times* in 1999, string players dressed this way risk having their audience become more fascinated with their jiggling flesh than with their music. Pianists and other instrumentalists can have the same problem when their upper arms are exposed, even if they are young and in generally good physical condition. When you are performing, make sure that what you wear is flattering to your own body. Use clothing to minimize your least attractive physical attributes and to downplay extremes in height and weight.

Color is also something to think about. We each look our best in certain colors. Some colors, such as pastels, may make you look washed out under stage lights, while bright colors may appear too loud. Black is always a safe choice because it looks dignified and strong, and does not vie for attention. Just because an outfit is black, however, does not mean that it is appropriately dressy or formal enough for the occasion. Casual clothes that are black still look like casual clothes.

As a musician, you may not feel qualified to choose the best clothing for yourself; your aesthetic sensibility may be largely aural and not visual. You may not feel sure about choosing styles, fabrics, and colors. Do not hesitate to get help when deciding on your concert wardrobe. If you do not know someone who has a special knack for dressing well, consider hiring a professional consultant. Work to get the confidence that results from knowing you look good onstage.

In the long run, what you really want people to notice and to remember is your playing. Performers with long professional careers eventually adopt a conservative and modest way of dressing that does not distract their audience.

Dressing for Utility and Comfort

A pair of good, comfortable shoes.

—Birgit Nilsson (b. 1918), Wagnerian soprano [in answer to the question, "What does it take to sing Wagnerian opera?"]

Performers need to consider more than just style. It is essential that there be nothing annoying or uncomfortable about your clothes. First, they should not be too tight. In addition to restricting the natural movement of your body, tight clothing can appear even tighter under stage lighting, which will create shadows around any underlying body contours or underwear. You also need to be able to move freely without worrying that your clothing will shift into undesirable positions. High slits on skirts, for example, are problematic in this way, as are shoulder straps (although bare arms are not recommended) and ill-fitting cummerbunds.

Concert clothes should fit comfortably. There should be enough room in the arms and back of your outfit to move as much as you need to move. Find a tailor you can rely on to keep your stage clothes fitting and looking just right. If you gain or lose a few pounds, get new clothes.

Nothing about your attire should need recurring attention, because adjusting your clothing onstage looks awkward and self-conscious. While performing, you want to be able to forget about your outfit entirely and bring your full concentration to the music. Therefore, never perform in clothing that you have not worn while playing your instrument, singing, or conducting. There is a good reason for a "dress" rehearsal even if you are performing solo.

Hem Lengths, Footwear, and Hosiery

When playing on a stage that is set up higher than the audience, do not fail to consider what you look like from the knees down. A skirt that may appear modest when people are standing at your level, may look outrageous from the first few rows of the orchestra. Short skirts are generally too revealing from a raised stage. Midcalf is about as short as a skirt can be without becoming a distraction. If the skirt is made of a material that may look sheer under stage lights, wear a dark-colored slip almost as long as the skirt, and always check beforehand to make sure it does not show below the hemline whatever your position.

Skirts shorter than full length, and all trousers, reveal glimpses of hosiery. Therefore, consider hosiery carefully as an asset to your overall appearance. It should be as dressy as the rest of your clothing and should not be lighter in color than your outfit or your skin. Allowing the audience to see above your hosiery, a fashion faux pas in any context, looks awful under stage lighting, especially if you have pale skin. Cellists in particular must be careful about this.

Long sleeves are best when hemmed to the correct length so they do not look too short or too long and do not get in your way. They should be plain and tapered toward the wrist, without any extra decorations such as fur, lace, or flashy cufflinks.

Choose your shoes carefully. It is best to have shoes that you use only for performing. Wear a style and color that coordinate appropriately with the rest of your outfit. Do not let shoes become worn or dirty, and keep them impeccably polished. Make sure you can walk in your shoes with a

Figure 2.1.   Bare Skin over Hosiery Looks Sloppy Onstage.

natural stride and without making too much noise on the stage. It is helpful not only to include shoes in your dress rehearsal, but also to walk and to practice in them until they really become part of you. Soles of new shoes should be roughed up enough so that they will not be slippery on a polished floor.

If you perform standing up, shoes with adequate support will keep you from being in pain or fatigued by the end of the concert. Just as you want to be able to forget about your clothes, you want to be able to forget about your footwear. Very high heels or stacked shoes may require the wearer to adopt an unnatural posture while walking, standing, and even sitting. The athletic aspect of musicianship requires the body to be in the best alignment for its most efficient performance. Although those with very short legs may find that high heels can help them sit in a more balanced way by allowing their feet to reach the floor, taller players can look downright silly in high heels when sitting. Be a musician first, and allow comfort and the natural use of your body, rather than fashion, to dictate your footwear.

Necklines, Hair, Makeup, and Accessories

Just as some audience members are sitting below you in the orchestra level, others will be sitting above you when you play in a hall with a balcony. Low necklines that appear modest under normal circumstances can become revealing when viewed from the upper levels of the hall. Consider also the appearance of a low neckline when bowing, the moment

Figure 2.2. Long-Legged Performers May Require Low-Heeled Shoes.

that the entire audience effectively sees you from above. Carefully choose your neckline so that it will not constitute a distraction.

Perform with your hair under control, so that the audience can have a clear, full view of your face. Your hair should be either short enough or securely fastened so that it does not obstruct this view. As with clothing, constantly touching your hair and moving it around can look sloppy, insecure, and self-conscious. Hair falling into your face during the cadenza can interfere with your concentration and make the audience wonder how you are going to deal with it. In addition, long hair that is not pulled back often projects too casual or seductive an appearance when you are wearing dressy clothes.

Ballet dancers and ice skaters learn to take care of their hair so that it stays in one place throughout their rigorous routines. Noticing how they do this can be instructive for musicians, who also need their hair to look neat and to stay put. Making sure your hair is well groomed can contribute greatly to your confidence onstage.

Wear understated makeup. It is a mistake to think that makeup must be overdone onstage. Just as in daily life, too much makeup attracts attention. Wear only clear nail polish and keep fingernails very short for playing an instrument.

When it comes to accessories, the fewer the better. It is best not to wear anything on your wrists or fingers if you are playing an instrument. That includes a watch, since the only reason to do so is to check the time, and you would not want the audience to see you do that. Be careful wearing hair ornaments that may come loose. A brooch or a necklace may be all right if your instrument never touches it. Certain instrumentalists, such as cellists and harpists, must consider the buttons on the front of their clothing, making certain that they are not in the way as they perform.

Scarves and shawls can be a nuisance and a distraction when they move around, as can eyeglasses. If you wear eyeglasses, have them adjusted to fit snugly so that they do not ride down your nose. Whatever you wear, practice performing while wearing it and make sure nothing in your wardrobe will demand your attention or your adjustment during the concert.

Dress to Enhance Your Performance

The best concert attire may be very different from what you would choose to wear for other occasions. Performers need to take many things into consideration that are not necessarily important in everyday life, such as how an outfit looks from odd angles and under bright lights, and whether it competes with the music for the attention of the audience.

In addition, the athletic aspect of musical performance requires concert clothes to be as comfortable as a sports uniform designed for a specific function. Anything less will distract the performer, who needs every bit of concentration to do the best job. As elements of comfort and utility, shoes, hairstyles, and accessories are as important as the clothing itself.

RAISE EXPECTATIONS WITH YOUR ENTRANCE

The moment you walk onstage, you make a strong impression on the audience based on your attitude and degree of confidence as reflected in your walk, facial expression, bow, and ability to create a meaningful silence before the first note is sounded. With these various elements of your entrance, you actually provide the audience with an expectation of the performance to come, positive or negative. It is in the interest of every performer to maximize the audience's high expectation before the first note is sounded. Attending to all the aspects of your entrance allows you to look enthusiastic, confident, and ready to perform.

Walking Onstage

Plan the route you will take from backstage to the place where you will stop and bow. Always enter from stage right (the audience's left side), unless there is something about the configuration of the building that prevents your doing so. Practice walking out onto the stage of every new venue so you get a feel for the distance and know about any detours or obstacles ahead of time.

For an actor, establishing a distinctive walk is an important element in the development of any character; actors learn that the way people walk says a great deal about them. When you walk onto a concert stage, the walk itself gives the audience a strong message about who you are, how you feel about being there, your attitude toward the audience, your level of enthusiasm for the performance, and even *whether or not you are a good performer*. It is in your best interest to give the audience as many positive messages about yourself as possible. The moment they see you they begin to form an opinion of how you will eventually play. If you can make them think that you are about to give them a good experience, chances are that they *will* have a good experience. The opposite is also true—negative expectations are usually fulfilled as well.

You want your walk to project enthusiastic anticipation for the event about to take place, as if you are going somewhere you want to go. The pace should therefore be purposeful without being hurried. Walking too quickly can look nervous and self-conscious. Walking too slowly can convey reluctance, a lack of enthusiasm, or simply a bad attitude.

Your body should look composed and relaxed with good, alert posture, arms naturally at your sides if not carrying an instrument. If you are carrying an instrument, make sure you are doing it in a professional and formal manner.

Some performers look at the audience as they are walking out, the way contestants in beauty pageants are instructed to walk onstage. Since walking in one direction while looking in another is not something we do in daily life, it is a challenge to make this look natural. The advantage of walking on in this way is that you will establish eye contact with your audience the moment they first see you, and you can maintain this rapport from the time you step onto the stage until your bow. Otherwise, you may look at where you are going as you normally would, and promptly take your position for your introductory bow.

In either case, know ahead of time exactly where that place is on the stage so you will not look in any way unsure of where you are going. It is sometimes a good idea to mark the spot on the stage with a piece of tape so you do not worry about finding it. Be conscious of making a visual picture as you take your bow. If you are playing on an instrument that is already there (piano, harp, percussion), stand so that the audience will see you and the instrument as a single unit. Getting close to where you will actually play will keep you from having to walk another distance after you bow, which can look anticlimactic and interrupt the timing of your entrance.

Facing the Audience

Now you have made your entrance. As the audience applauds, you arrive at the spot onstage upon which you will stop and bow. As you face the audience, your facial expression should complete the impression given by your walk. The audience should feel that you are happy to see them and appreciative that they took the time and trouble to be there. Genuine sincerity goes right to the heart of your audience. You can convey good feelings more effectively by making eye contact with a single audience member toward the back of the orchestra section or in the lowest balcony, or by letting your eyes unhurriedly sweep from one side of the back of the audience to the other.

Smiling is good, but again, your smile must be sincere to establish rapport with your audience. We have all seen photos of people with fake smiles plastered on their faces. An audience can recognize such a smile from a great distance, and they will immediately see that it is phony. The performer must truly have a good attitude and positive feelings. Besides, cultivating such feelings as you greet your audience is the best way to break down boundaries between you and them, to settle yourself, to demystify the situation, and to get ready to play. It also effectively reduces preconcert jitters. Try imagining that you are smiling at someone you love, or meeting your best friend at the airport after a long absence.

Bowing

Bowing to the audience is like shaking hands with an individual—a proper formal greeting and introduction. Establishing eye contact both before and after the bow conveys sincerity. Come onto the stage and move purposefully to the spot where you will perform. Then:

1. Stop and look out at the audience, establishing eye contact.
2. Bow.
3. Stand back up and stay in that spot until you have reestablished eye contact with the audience.

Failing to do all three things is equivalent to meeting someone and shaking hands without eye contact, or turning to walk away before the handshake is finished—either of which would be dismissive and rude.

Bow with your feet together, because keeping feet apart can look disorganized and awkward. Keep your shoulders down and your hands relaxed at your sides unless holding your instrument. Pianists may touch the piano with the left hand as they bow. Lower your eyes to the floor as you bend from the waist—gently, with no jerky motions (never "throw" your hair)—to about a 45-degree angle. Lowering your eyes indicates humility and respect. Maintaining eye contact during the actual bow is either threatening (the kind of bow used toward opponents in the martial arts) or immodest, and therefore is not recommended in musical performance.

Move your head and body together as you bow without sticking out your chin or going down chin first. Keep your hands in one place at your sides and do not let them ride down your legs or dangle out in front of you.

An unbuttoned suit jacket separates and appears untidy when bowing, and will allow a long tie, if not fastened with a tie tack, to fall straight down perpendicular to your body. After your first bow, you may inconspicuously unbutton before playing to give yourself full freedom of movement and to keep the jacket from puckering unattractively as you play; refasten as you get ready to bow at the end. If you perform wearing a suit jacket, practice quick and unobtrusive buttoning and unbuttoning without having to look down as you do it.

Nothing about the bow should appear hurried. Take your time coming to your place and looking at the audience both before and after the bow.

Figure 2.3.   A Disorganized Bow Projects a Lack of Confidence.

Also take your time moving into playing position, all the while maintaining a sincere and pleasing facial expression. By entering unhurriedly, yet intentionally, you are drawing the audience into your own sense of time and space; you will be turning your attention to your instrument as the audience is settling down after having applauded your entrance. By setting the pace in this way, you can prepare for the concert together with the audience, and by this time, you have given them a number of positive impressions of yourself and positive expectations for your ensuing performance.

Assuming Playing Position

You and the audience are now getting ready together to hear the music. At this transition point in a performance, it is important to maintain an atmosphere of respect as you turn your attention to your instrument. The respectful and anticipatory mood that your entrance and bow have created can be completely undone by stopping to tune your instrument at this crucial moment. It is best to have already tuned before coming onstage. This can be accomplished with the use of an electronic tuning device that may be tuned to the piano ahead of time. If performing without a piano, there is no reason to tune onstage at all; tune backstage, out of hearing of the audience. If you must do any tuning onstage, do it as quickly, quietly, and unobtrusively as possible. No long riffs that sound like practicing or showing off; no endless zeroing in on the pitches. Nothing can break the spell you have created for the audience like tuning. The first sound they should hear is the first note on your program.

Never turn your back to the audience unless you are the conductor or any player who, for whatever reason, must actually perform facing the back of the stage. Get ready quickly, but with composure. If the stage personnel have done their job, you should not need to arrange stage furnishings in any way (move chairs, raise or lower the piano lid, change the height of the stand, adjust the piano bench, position the stand).

Take a few moments to create a total silence filled with your intense concentration. Performers who are good at this can focus the entire audience within this silence before they begin to play, creating the ideal atmosphere in which to sound the first notes of their piece.

When performing with an accompanist, make sure you have rehearsed the beginning of the piece with the least amount of demonstrative counting, either verbal or physical. The beginning should look very smooth to the audience, as if you are simply breathing together.

Practicing and Assessing Your Entrance and Bow

Entering and bowing is an art in itself, and few people do it well without extensive thought and repetitive practice. In earlier times, performers had to rely on the mirror and on the opinions of others to assess their entrances and bows and to work on improving them. But now we have the video camera, an invaluable tool for musicians wishing to study their stage presence. Even the most practiced professionals will be surprised upon observing their own performance by how their entrances, exits, and bows may diverge from the image they have of themselves in their mind's eye. Studying yourself in this way is the beginning of a positive change that is bound to improve your overall image. If you find that you are having trouble on your own making the changes you think you need to make, you may benefit from working with a specialist in the art of stage presence or with an acting coach to create the best possible initial impression for your audience.

DURING THE PERFORMANCE

One can correct facial grimaces by placing a mirror on the reading desk of the spinet or harpsichord.

—François Couperin (1668–1733), composer, harpsichordist, organist

As you play, keep the audience focused on the music as much as possible by not giving them other things to notice and think about. Body language should demonstrate intense, yet calm, concentration. You need to be aware of potential problems in this area so you may play with composure and, after playing, graciously accept the audience's applause.

Annoying Physical Habits

As they practice, most musicians acquire physical habits that can be distracting in performance. Intense effort and concentration, for example, may create an unpleasant, even grotesque, facial expression. A strong sense of rhythm or of melody may produce body movement that is overblown and intrusive.

Some performers do the same things over and over, more from habit than necessity, creating behaviors that are difficult to overlook when the

Figure 2.4.   A Tense Facial Expression May Make the Performer Appear Angry or Disdainful.

audience is trying to listen to the music. These behaviors fall into three categories:

Personal Habits

Mopping your brow
Wringing or flexing your hands or fingers
Wiping your mouth
Licking your lips
Tapping your toes
Adjusting your hair
Touching your eyeglasses
Breathing audibly
Humming as you play

Handling Your Instrument

Shaking out moisture
Applying rosin to the bow
Pulling loose hairs from the bow
Wiping the keyboard
Rattling the valves
Audibly blowing into a mouthpiece or horn
Licking the reed

Dramatic Gestures

Assuming a tense or overblown facial expression
Tossing your head
Flailing your arms
Swaying your body
Bobbing your head
"Dancing" to the music

Some of these behaviors may be perfectly all right when they are necessary for the well-being of the performer and instrument, or when dictated by aspects of the piece. When they are repetitive and predictable, however, and appear pointless, they become distracting or even annoying.

Just as the best and most seasoned performers tend to dress conservatively to avoid calling attention to themselves, they have also learned to adopt a poised demeanor and to maintain quiet concentration as they play and during rests. It is the same kind of concentration that they have used to bring the audience into their silence at the beginning of the piece.

When there is accompaniment, it is important for the soloist to be mentally performing whenever the accompanist is playing alone, from the first note to the very last note of every piece. While concentrating in this way, be careful not to react to any mistakes the accompanist makes.

Perspiration

Some performers perspire excessively as they perform and need to use a handkerchief to dry their face and hands between pieces or during rests. The handkerchief should be folded, pressed, and kept that way; do not unfurl the handkerchief or wad it up. Blot, not wipe, your skin.

Give some attention to how you will carry the handkerchief and where you will place it during the performance. You should not dig it out from a trousers pocket. It is more easily accessible from an interior jacket pocket or from inside a long sleeve. Pianists may carry the handkerchief in the hand and place it inside the piano before they begin to play.

A white handkerchief will glare under stage lights. A subdued color, one that does not clash with the color of your attire, is better.

Never wipe your hands on your clothing. You may be doing this unconsciously. If you are not in the habit of having a handkerchief with you when you perform, notice what you do whenever your hands become moist.

If perspiration is a problem, wear colors and fabrics that will minimize the appearance of moisture. Nonshiny fabrics and very dark colors are best.

Eye Contact

Instrumentalists should not look directly at the audience as they perform. In fact, the only time to make eye contact with the audience is immediately before and immediately after the bow (unless you also choose to establish eye contact as you are walking onstage). Constant or furtive eye contact both during the actual playing and during rests will make you look self-conscious. Do, however, allow the audience to see your face as you play by making sure that nothing, such as your music stand or your hairstyle, obstructs the audience's view. Be sure to hold your head up if you play a guitar or cello or the audience will see only the top of your head.

Depending on the work being performed, singers are required either to address the audience directly or to remain detached as an instrumentalist would. In either case, the singer must be aware of exactly what the music requires in this regard and consciously decide whether to establish eye contact with the audience. Singers must be careful not to hold their score in front of their face, but flat and low in front of them.

Reacting to Mistakes

Always assume that every performance will have mistakes. Much more important than eliminating all mistakes (which is virtually impossible) is how you react to them. Do not allow the audience to get worried about your mistakes. It is imperative that you eliminate even the tiniest reaction, in either your face or body. Visibly reacting to mistakes makes them seem much worse than they are. We can follow the example of ice skaters: performers who have learned to rise from a fall on the ice with a big smile, almost as if they had actually *intended* to fall.

Keeping your composure during and after a mistake is very difficult for some players. Whether they realize it or not, most musicians actually practice *losing* composure by allowing themselves histrionics in the privacy of the practice room and then, once onstage, find it impossible to change this lifelong, ingrained bad habit. Be aware of the ways that you handle mistakes as you practice and eliminate any reaction that your audience may be able to see.

Playing from Memory

You should have the score in your head, and not your head in the score.

—Hans von Bülow (1830–1894), conductor

Most of the major conductors, great pianists, and other legendary soloists performed almost exclusively from memory. There is no question that playing from memory, without having to bother with the printed score at all, is the preferable way to perform. This way, you securely know every note of the music and thus totally avoid the potentially messy business of dealing with the score on stage. But practical considerations force most performers to resort to using their music at least some of the time. When music must be used during a performance, how can it be done with the least possible distraction?

As much as possible, you want the audience to remain unaware of the score. With the exception of singers, who may hold the score in their hands as they sing, soloists should never have to carry their music or the music stand onto the stage as they walk out to play. The score and stand should have been positioned beforehand by stage personnel (or by you before the audience arrives) and opened to the first page. The height of the music stand also should be preset so that you will not need to adjust it in front of your audience before you begin. You should not have to carry the score or stand off with you when you are done.

The score should remain completely hidden by the music stand. If you have a particularly wide or high score, or have taped copied pages together

Figure 2.5.   Keep Your Music from Spilling over the Stand.

to avoid difficult page turns, it is wise to purchase an extension or an expandable stand, making it wide or high enough to accommodate the size of the pages. Use only a score in good condition, and make sure to take care of any single pages that could fall during the concert. Always carry clips with you, and if you need to fasten the score to the stand, do it. Never turn pages in a demonstrative or sudden manner, but rather as unobtrusively and quietly as possible.

Know the music as thoroughly as possible. Use the score as a general guideline and refrain from reading the music note by note during a performance. Such intense reading takes your focus away from your surroundings and turns it instead to the page, which can make it look as if you are practicing. Follow Hans von Bülow's advice and have the score in your head—not your head in the score.

ACKNOWLEDGING APPLAUSE

Carefully rehearse your body language and your concentration to control the timing of the audience's applause at the end of your piece. Even the most unsophisticated audience can be dissuaded from clapping between movements or too early in the significant silence at the end of a piece by the way the performer maintains concentration and holds the body. Invite the applause to begin exactly when you want it by releasing your concentration, both mentally and physically.

As the applause begins, stand to bow as you did at the beginning, with the same relaxed facial expression and eye contact with your audience. If you feel drained and exhausted, do not show it. Bow with sincere gratitude toward the listeners. Accept the compliment of applause openly and graciously, avoiding any hint of a fake, "aw-shucks" modesty. If you turn your head even slightly during the bow, you run the risk of projecting this undesirable impression.

Decide beforehand how and when you will leave the stage. You may decide to bow two or three times before leaving if the applause is particularly enthusiastic and to leave after the first bow if it is not. Walk off with good posture and at a brisk but not hurried pace. Stay offstage or return quickly for another bow. It is important to come out for additional bows while the applause is at a peak and not already dying down. Avoid milking the applause by coming back too many times. It is always best to leave before the audience asks you to leave.

ENCORES

Although encores may look like a spontaneous response to an audience's enthusiasm, the performer has, of course, carefully planned one or more of them ahead of time. You need to know exactly what you will play as if it is part of your printed program. Just as you never want to take too many bows, you never want to play too many encores. Leave the audience always wanting a little more, rather than run the risk of playing too long.

If you want to play an encore as part of your program, come back onstage quickly after the first or second bow and get into position to perform again right away. Announce the name of the piece in a clear voice as soon as the audience is still. It is almost always appropriate to add one piece in this way. Performing multiple encores is all right, as long as the audience remains enthusiastic. Avoid teasing your audience by making them wonder whether or not you will play again, and do not make them beg as you repeatedly enter, bow, and leave the stage. Either play or end the concert without being coy. Too few encores are better than too many.

TALKING TO YOUR AUDIENCE

There are times when you may want to address the audience during the course of a performance—to break down barriers between musician and concertgoer, introduce yourself to the audience, or present additional information that may not appear in the program, for example. Only those performers who are good public speakers should attempt this, being aware that the formality of a traditional concert is significantly lowered whenever you take on the added role of narrator or host.

If informality is not the goal, a preconcert talk or interview followed by an intermission is often the solution that allows musicians to address the audience while at the same time preserving the formal character of the subsequent concert. To further draw the distinction between talking and performing, it is best not to talk in your concert attire, but to change clothes between the talk and the performance. Publicizing such talks ahead of time, and holding them before the scheduled time of the beginning of the performance, also makes it possible for audience members to skip the verbal presentation if they wish.

PERFORMING WITH OTHERS

If you have an accompanist, be sure that both of you practice exits, entrances, and bows together. It looks good if you, as the soloist, are generous in your public recognition of your accompanist. If you are equal collaborators, come on and off the stage as equals (soloist in the lead coming on and accompanist in the lead going off) and bow together. If the accompanist is performing a subordinate role in the music, it is appropriate for the soloist to be in the lead walking both on and off and to bow alone. With a gesture, the soloist may invite the accompanist to take his or her individual bow at the end of the concert. Always exit the stage together, single file and at the same pace. After the first exit, subsequent bows may be taken by the soloist alone.

When soloing with an ensemble of singers or musicians, your entrances, exits, and bows will be coordinated with the conductor. In the case of a conductorless ensemble, you must come on and off the stage and bow together with the group. In either case, since a performing organization may have a distinctive style or pace of entering, leaving, and bowing, it is appropriate to request a short rehearsal for these maneuvers so that they appear organized during the concert. The details of repeated bowing, acknowledgment of individual players or sections, encores, and so forth should all be decided ahead of time.

KEEP YOUR AUDIENCE FROM BEGINNING TO END

As you perform, encourage your audience to concentrate on the sound of the music by eliminating as many potential distractions as you can. These include repetitive and unnecessary physical habits, facial contortions, inappropriately looking at the audience, visibly reacting to mistakes, and fumbling with the score. At the conclusion of a performance, acknowledge applause in a professional and rehearsed manner, always making your final bow while the audience remains animated. Plan encores to avoid the anticlimactic feeling that results from playing too many of them.

ATTEND TO ALL ASPECTS OF YOUR STAGE PRESENCE

Your job is not over when the music is ready to be performed. Have you done everything possible to maximize your appearance and demeanor when you perform? Time and effort must be spent on many aspects of stage presence so that your music can be heard in the best possible context. Choose the most appropriate clothes for the event and for the task at hand. Study and practice your entrance and bow so that the audience will anticipate a good performance before you even begin. Evaluate your behavior onstage for anything that your audience will find distracting. Practice *not* reacting to mistakes. Either perform from memory, or make sure that your use of the score is as unobtrusive as possible. Accept applause graciously, and always leave the audience wanting more.

Your hard work deserves to be displayed in the best light. Constantly evaluate your stage presence as it is today, and work toward improving it in the future. Your audience will notice and appreciate your attention to this important, yet neglected aspect of performance.

**LIST 2.1   PERFORMERS: AVOID DOING
THESE THINGS ONSTAGE**

- Turning your back to the audience (unless you perform in this position)
- Chewing gum or holding anything in your mouth
- Adjusting your clothing or hair
- Touching your eyeglasses
- Scratching an itch
- Wearing distracting or uncomfortable clothes
- Wearing noisy shoes or shoes that make it difficult to walk or play your instrument naturally
- Wearing anything on the arms, wrists, or fingers
- Keeping time with movements of your body (unless you are the conductor)
- Arranging stage furnishings (piano lid, stands, chairs, and so on)

Chapter 3

The Page Turner

Ever since performers (especially keyboard players, who usually play continuously throughout a piece) have begun to appear before audiences, they have wanted to solve the thorny problem of how to turn pages while also playing their instrument. The nineteenth-century pianist and conductor Sir Charles Hallé developed a mechanical page-turning apparatus for pianists that was operated by the player's foot. It was reported at the time, however, that audiences became so fascinated watching the clever device in action that they forgot to pay attention to the music. Similar mechanical inventions over the years have met their demise for the same reason. (Very recently, a digital music stand has come on the market that stores a part or a score electronically. "Pages" are "turned" at the touch of the performer's finger or toe. As yet, however, there has been no ideal replacement for the human page turner.)

Even if the performer is adept at turning pages, for difficult music it is still a good idea to have a person onstage to assist. The sheer physical feat of being able to turn pages and play at the same time can have the same effect on the audience as the mechanical devices. The person turning pages onstage is an important element in the overall presentation of the concert. When you are that person, in addition to turning pages at the right time you can actively contribute to the stage presence of the entire performance.

APPEARANCE

General dress guidelines that apply to performers apply to page turners as well. Be especially careful about loose-fitting sleeves and dangly jewelry

Figure 3.1.   The Page Turner Can Seriously Detract from a Performance.

that may get in the way of the performer, and always avoid the use of perfumed personal products, especially when working with singers or wind
players. Your attire can be somewhat less formal and less colorful than the
others', but never casual.

You should never have any candy, lozenges, or gum in your mouth.
Everyone knows that actually chewing gum is out of the question, but
many appear to believe that they can hold things in their mouths unobtrusively. This is not true, especially onstage.

If possible, attend one or more rehearsals, or at least take the time to
read through the scores together with the performer, making sure you
know about all repeats and cuts and can easily understand everything in
the music. Some players mark the exact beat on which they will want
every page turned. The performer should never have to give cues with the
head or body when a page needs turning.

ENTRANCES

On entering the stage, you should walk behind the performers and go directly to the piano or other music stand, without looking at the audience
or acknowledging the applause in any way. Move in a relaxed and purposeful manner, at the same pace as the other musicians, with head up
and eyes forward. Reach your designated place on the stage just before
the musicians bow.

Carry the score onstage, closed and at your side. Place it on the desk, open to the first page. Locate the first page of the piece before coming onstage so you will not have to look for it in front of the audience.

You may remove the score from the stage when finished. This may be necessary if there are several different performers in one concert. But if there is nothing about the concert that requires bringing the score on and off, it can be placed on the desk before the audience arrives and left there as you leave the stage with the performers. It looks neater if you close the score and lay it down on the flat part of the desk before leaving.

DURING THE PERFORMANCE

Your chair is best situated slightly behind the pianist's bench on the upstage side. If the chair is just next to the pianist, it will be in the way. Sit upstage of other soloists if you are turning their pages as well. Be sure your chair is not too low and that it does not squeak.

Remain seated between page turns and stand to turn pages. It is best to turn *all* the pages, not just certain ones. Keep in mind that repeatedly standing up and sitting down throughout a performance is potentially very distracting if not done in the most unobtrusive and smooth manner. Thus, you should have no trouble physically standing up and sitting down in a controlled, quiet manner.

Before, during, and after the performance, sit up with good posture and both feet on the floor. Remain absolutely still (but not stiff), concentrating on the music. Keep your eyes always on the score, never looking at the players, the audience, or around the room. Your hands should remain quiet and relaxed in your lap. Prepare pages by flaring their upper right-hand corners so the pages can be easily separated and you will not be tempted to moisten your fingers with your tongue. Turn pages efficiently and quietly—never moving any part of your body to the music (e.g., bobbing your head or tapping your toes).

EXIT

During the first bow at the end of the concert, remain seated, looking at the score, and then rise promptly to follow the performers as they go offstage. Always turn toward, not away, from the audience. Remain offstage during subsequent bows unless your presence is required during the performance of an encore. Ask to be included in rehearsals for entrances, exits, and bows, including those for possible encores.

DO MORE THAN JUST TURN PAGES

Realize that much depends on your role as page turner. If you do not dress appropriately, the look of the other performers will be compromised. The audience will be distracted if you move around too much or if you are not fully concentrating on the music. Entrances and exits will appear disorganized if you have not rehearsed your part in them. Be aware of all the ways that you can contribute to a successful performance.

Chapter 4

The Small Ensemble
(No Conductor)

When collaborating with another musician or other musicians without the direction of a conductor, who is in charge of your stage presence—i.e., how are decisions affecting your stage presence made? Your appearance on stage can be greatly improved by consciously planning the various aspects of your presentation.

When there are two or more musicians on a stage performing together, it helps the audience to be drawn into your music when you *look* like a polished ensemble even before you begin to play and *sound* like one. Therefore, you want to look as if you have thought about all aspects of your appearance, including attire, equipment, your way of moving together on and off the stage, and your way of acknowledging applause.

Although you may consider yourselves to have a collaborative rather than a hierarchical relationship with one another, it is a good idea for any pair or group of musicians, after deciding major policies together, to identify an individual or individuals who may take a proprietary interest in your organization's stage presence. There may be someone who enjoys choosing and inspecting your attire, who may like to clean and repair your stage furnishings, or who would be interested in conducting rehearsals for your exits, entrances, and bows. Once these people have been identified, give them the authority to carry out the wishes of the entire ensemble in such matters. Without having individuals who take the responsibility for maintaining the level of its stage presence, any ensemble will become increasingly disorganized, because there is no one consistently taking care of the details.

ATTIRE

Duos and other small ensembles often perform in intimate halls or in rooms where the musicians' attire will come under scrutiny by the audience. If anyone's clothing is not in good condition, freshly cleaned, and pressed, people will notice. It will also be obvious if outfits do not fit well or if shoes are worn and scuffed. Someone in the group should be assigned to conduct inspections for grooming and the general condition of everyone's clothes. This may be as far as you can go when playing in an ensemble that may not regularly perform together.

It takes planning to determine a level of formality that you wish to achieve, and then to make sure all members look that way. The most common faux pas in a performing ensemble's way of dressing is incongruity in style and formality. Within a single performing organization, it is not unusual to see some musicians dressed as if for a black-tie occasion, some looking as if they are going to work in an office, and still others who would fit in at a folk festival. It is also common to see one or more members of a group who dress in a way that calls undue attention to themselves, taking attention away from the group. Even when there are only two of you, a pianist and another instrument for example, it is important to coordinate your clothes.

The easiest way to prevent incongruities and attention-getting attire is to have a uniform outfit designed for all members. If you dress yourselves individually, without the benefit of a strict dress code or an actual uniform, it will appear as if you have not given thought to the way you are dressing as a group—and, truly, you have not. There can be a different design for men and women, but without stipulating exactly what everyone will wear, the ensemble will constantly be grappling with the issue of how to appear as if it has thoughtfully planned its attire. The organization can devise a clear dress code and strictly enforce it, but will find, in the long run, that having a uniform is easier and will produce better results. To adapt your look for different venues, seasons, and times of day, a variety of uniforms for various occasions may be chosen.

Whether designing a uniform or creating a dress code, include every aspect of the musicians' outfit, including accessories and shoes. Just one musician wearing brown socks when everyone else is wearing black can distract an audience.

Begin to raise awareness among your members about issues of group attire by taking time to observe video recordings of yourselves while performing. Also, discuss the way you presently dress—together, you will come up with good ideas for constructive change. Consciously decide how you really want to look, and begin taking steps to reach your goal.

EQUIPMENT

The total impression you make on your audience is enhanced by your use of equipment, such as chairs and music stands that are uniform in style and in new condition. The best professional ensembles, realizing the importance of this, go to the trouble of bringing their own equipment with them to every place they perform. Often, some members of the ensemble will require a chair of a certain height or configuration (such as a particularly low piano bench or a cello chair) or a music stand that opens extra wide. Do not expect to find these things in most performing venues. Makeshift solutions, such as using two nesting chairs to raise the seat or placing two music stands side by side to make one wider stand, look slipshod and reveal a lack of planning and apparent general indifference to the details and requisites of your performance. Always assume, unless you know for certain otherwise, that you will need to bring your own equipment to all performances, and be committed to maintaining uniform-looking equipment in new condition.

ENSEMBLE MANEUVERS ONSTAGE

Without frequent rehearsals of your entrances, bows, exits, and the way in which you wish to begin pieces and acknowledge applause together, your spontaneous way of doing these things will look disorganized. The more members in your ensemble, the higher the potential that you will look unconnected and lost onstage. Here is another area where careful study of yourselves on video can be very instructive, revealing all manner of details that you may not have considered.

Walking Onstage

This may seem simple enough, but the way you all walk onstage as a group projects a certain image of yourselves. Every ensemble can decide ahead of time exactly what image it wants to project and then can practice an entrance that will have the desired effect. You will want to come out together, which means that you should all walk at the same pace without bunching up or leaving big gaps between people. All players should have finished walking before any begin to bow so that you all bow together. All players, to minimize movement onstage after the bow, should bow as close as possible to the spot where they will eventually perform. The order in which you walk out will be determined in this way by your position on the stage where you play. If you walk out in a different order, you

Figure 4.1.   Makeshift Solutions Reflect Poor Planning and Inattention to Detail.

will need to move around too much, crossing in front of or behind each other. For this reason, it is probably best not to revert to traditional rules of etiquette for your entrance, such as having women enter before men or elders precede younger players.

Be conscious of entering with good posture, erect without being stiff, looking poised and eager to perform. If you all adopt a similar facial expression, you can portray an ensemble attitude, rather than a motley collection of individuals. For those who walk out carrying their instruments, add to the look of uniformity by coordinating how you will hold them.

Do not carry your music with you as you come onstage. Arrange parts on the music stands ahead of time, before the audience arrives, or have them placed there by stage personnel, open to the first page of the music. Adjust the exact position of each stand (height, angle, tilt) and chair beforehand as well so that players will not need to make any of these adjustments in front of the audience.

Bowing

Before making the actual bow, all members should have come to a complete stop and be facing the audience, standing with good posture and feet together, and making eye contact with the audience. Practice bowing at the same pace: after making eye contact with the audience together for the same amount of time, all bend down to the same angle (about 45 degrees from perpendicular) with eyes lowered to the feet; stay down together for a slow count of three, then come back up and reestablish eye contact with the audience before moving into your playing positions. If you do not plan your bows to this degree of detail, some musicians in the group will draw attention by doing something different from the others. By bowing more quickly than others, for example, or bending down much further than anyone else, tossing the hair, or failing to lower the eyes during the bow, individual members can undermine the desired appearance of purposeful and planned unity. Think of yourselves as an ensemble before and after you actually play—for the entire time you are in front of the audience.

Tuning

Tuning is best done beforehand and offstage, where the audience cannot hear you. An electronic tuning device is useful when you must tune to an instrument, usually a piano, already onstage. If for some reason tuning must be done onstage, do it as quietly and as unobtrusively as possible, having established ahead of time what pitches you will play. It is best, however, when the first sound the audience hears is the first note of the program.

DURING THE PERFORMANCE

In rehearsal, develop a way to begin each piece that will not be overly dramatic, using collective concentration and breathing. No conversation should ever be necessary among the musicians onstage. One member is usually designated to conduct the entrances, which are accomplished most successfully when all of the members are ready and concentrating together so that the audience is least aware of the mechanics of this process. Avoid any obvious counting, foot tapping, or head bobbing. As with solo musicians, ensembles appear most impressive when they play together with the least amount of visible effort.

Make sure there are no loose pages in your music that could fall off the stand during the performance. Turn pages gently and quietly. Avoid page turning during others' solos. Bring clips and tape and arrange your music in the order in which you will perform it. Do whatever is necessary to keep the printed music from becoming a distraction.

Never react to mistakes, your own or others'. Keep strong concentration during those times when you are not playing. Do not look around the room during long rests or relax your posture. The audience can tell when you are daydreaming. Remain a fully participating member of the ensemble at all times by concentrating on the music from beginning to end.

AT THE CONCLUSION OF THE CONCERT

Responding to applause and leaving the stage are other maneuvers that require rehearsal if they are to look smooth and planned. Someone in the group should be designated to give the others signals that tell them when to bow and when to leave the stage. When leaving, as well as when entering, everyone should move as a group, at the same pace and with uniform spacing. Avoid situations where some members are leaving while others are still bowing, or where some are bunching up because one person is moving at a slower pace than the group as a whole.

Also plan and rehearse reentrances for additional bows and encores so that your coordinated appearance is not compromised at the end of your concert. You may want to appear spontaneous after you have played, but actual spontaneity can result in a look of unprofessional confusion. Practice *looking* spontaneous while also planning your moves so that you will maintain the intentional look of your ensemble until you leave the stage for the last time. When invited to take an individual bow, accept the audience's recognition graciously and in a dignified manner, without inappropriate humility. Never visibly resist an invitation to bow alone or force another to beg you to bow.

Because there will be no time to make a collective decision, appoint one member to decide when the group will stop going back for additional bows. Do everything as a group. Do not allow one or two members to go back onstage and then coax the others to join them. Usually, by the time all of this happens, the audience has stopped applauding and the players are forced to leave the stage as the audience itself begins to leave. It is always best to stop coming out for bows while the audience is still at the peak of their enthusiasm in order to avoid milking the applause. Coordinate your final exit with the raising of the house lights as the stage goes dim.

EVALUATING YOUR STAGE PRESENCE

It is useful to study a video recording of a dress rehearsal or performance to improve details of your stage presence. Viewing yourselves from the audience's point of view can be very revealing, and is the first step necessary for positive change. Working with a professional consultant is often the best way for an ensemble to achieve a truly professional demeanor and appearance and to establish procedures that will maintain good stage presence in the future.

MAKING STAGE PRESENCE A PRIORITY IN YOUR ENSEMBLE

When small ensembles with no conductor ignore issues of stage presence, they run the risk of appearing disorganized and unprofessional. Performances of such groups too often look like rehearsals.

To project a polished and professional appearance, your ensemble must consciously plan attire, stage furnishings, and group entrances, exits, and bows. It is best to assign individuals specific stage presence duties and give them the authority to carry out these duties. By making an aspect of stage presentation part of each player's job description, awareness of stage presence issues among all members of the organization will be heightened.

Your audience may not realize why, but they will experience more exciting and satisfying performances as you work to improve the presentation of your ensemble.

LIST 4.1   WAYS TO KEEP YOUR PERFORMANCE FROM LOOKING LIKE A REHEARSAL

- Perform with furniture and equipment in new condition, without dust, dirt, scratches, or dents. (No ownership stencils on the back of your music stands!)
- Do not perform housekeeping duties onstage. Assign the moving and setting up of furniture, large instruments, stands, and scores to stagehands.
- Require stagehands to dress uniformly and not too casually.
- Coordinate the attire among members of the ensemble.
- Leave all personal items (purses, instrument cases, extra clothing) backstage. Carry nothing onstage but your instrument.
- Never turn your back to the audience.
- Refrain from talking to other musicians while onstage.
- Avoid excessive tuning or warming up within hearing of the audience.
- Avoid excessive, demonstrative, or predictable attention to your instrument during the performance (emptying water from winds, wiping, adjusting joints, applying rosin to a bow, pulling hair from a bow, cleaning or drying piano keys)
- Keep tempo with concentration, not by beating it with part of your body.
- Practice and rehearse enough so your eyes are not glued to the score.
- Turn pages silently and unobtrusively.
- Refrain from perceptibly reacting to mistakes (yours or others').
- Rehearse every detail of entrances, exits, and bows in the hall where the performance will take place.
- Establish eye contact with the audience immediately before and immediately after your bow.
- From the stage, do not look for, or signal to, friends in the audience before, during, or after the performance.
- Bring 100 percent of your concentration to the performance every second you are in front of the audience, whether you are playing or not.

Chapter 5

The Large Vocal Ensemble

A choir sounds no better than it looks.

— Paul Hill (1939–1999), choral conductor, composer, arranger

A chorus can look unified more easily than an instrumental ensemble because its members are all doing the same thing while standing together in the same way. There is also a strong tradition for singers in vocal ensembles to wear strictly uniform dress. Nevertheless, chorus members need clear and detailed guidelines for their onstage appearance and demeanor if the group is to make its stage presentation the best it can be. The goal of any chorus is to create, from many members, one single entity, or "voice." This is accomplished by enacting and maintaining policies designed to maximize the look of professionalism and poise in the ensemble, and by eliminating anything on the part of the individuals that may draw attention to themselves or away from the group.

Within the organization, individual personnel or committees may be assigned responsibility for certain aspects of stage presence, not only to set policy but also to enforce it.

DRESS

The ultimate in choral uniformity is a choir robe. In addition to being identical for everyone, male and female, it hangs attractively on individual bodies and frames all the singers' faces in exactly the same way. Because it is usually purchased from a single source or custom made, the material is also identical in color and texture from robe to robe. It is simple for singers to wear and adapts to all but the most radical changes in body size.

A chorus wearing robes portrays a certain image, but it may not be one you want for your ensemble. There are many other possible styles of dress, including formal black-tie attire, military uniforms, and various, more casual outfits. It is always preferable that everyone be wearing exactly the same thing. If singers are asked to provide their own clothes, the results will be less than optimum. If required to wear black trousers or skirts and white tops, for example, everyone will appear with different styles, some dressy and others not so. The necklines, sleeve lengths, hemlines, and fabrics will vary, and the assorted "whites" and "blacks" will not look the same onstage.

The best clothing for chorus members is either custom made or purchased from a single source where the chosen outfits will remain available. It may be decided that the women and men in the group wear different clothing, but then the desirability of creating two visually distinct groups of singers in the ensemble must be considered. It is possible, if custom made, for male and female attire to be designed in a gender-specific way and to look alike onstage.

Whatever the chosen outfit, it should be kept in good condition, clean, and pressed. It should fit well and not cling to the body. Choir robes should be adjusted to a uniform length for each singer.

Shoes and Hosiery

Uniform footwear is also preferable to having chorus members choose their own, especially for those singers in the front row (although the audience may see the feet of all the singers as they enter and exit the stage). Variety in footwear can undermine the uniform look achieved in the rest of the attire.

Consideration must be given to the comfort and support of shoes, since singers must stand for extended lengths of time and poor foot support may cause upper bodies to shift and sway.

Hair, Makeup, and Accessories

Require singers to wear their hair short enough so that it does not fall into their faces as they sing, or to fasten it back securely so that it will need no adjustment during a performance. Hairstyles, including mustaches and beards, should be congruent with the style of the clothing (not too casual) and appear well groomed.

Makeup should be understated. One or more singers with heavy makeup will look very different from all the others. It is best if no jewelry is worn, including rings (with the possible exception of wedding bands) and watches. If earrings are allowed, they should not dangle.

DEMEANOR

Develop guidelines for the singers' demeanor and circulate these among all members; devise as well a system of enforcement that may be applied strictly and fairly. The singers will appreciate being instructed in the principles of good stage presence and will know exactly what is expected of them.

Preconcert Preparation

Require singers to arrive well before the beginning of a performance so that they may make preparations in an unstressed environment and so that vocal warmups involving all members may be conducted backstage. It is bad for morale and for the performers' voices when some singers rush in at the last moment before a concert. Taking time to make preparations together will ensure that everyone is warmed up, thinking together, and feeling ready to perform. Before actually going out onstage, it is a good idea for the singers to observe a period of silence to prepare themselves mentally and to avoid finishing conversations or being otherwise preoccupied as they walk out in front of the audience.

Entrance

In rehearsal, the entrance of the chorus should have been practiced so that it will go as smoothly as possible at the concert. All singers should know exactly where they are going and who is walking ahead of them. Practice entering at a uniform pace, so that people do not bunch up or leave big gaps among themselves.

Take attendance before the concert. Remove chairs of absent members and plan how to fill in empty spots on risers.

Chorus members should enter promptly, walking directly to their places without looking around or at the audience. The singers should all adopt pleasant facial expressions during their entrance, as if looking forward to the concert. There should be no conversation or wordless communication with other chorus or audience members. When in place, the entire chorus may be seated on cue from a designated member and then rise on the entrance of the conductor.

Standing and sitting should be done exactly together. With practice, a large chorus can make the simple acts of standing up and sitting down appear very exciting to the audience and draw them into the group's discipline even before the music begins.

While Performing

All singers should be standing at a uniform angle. The angle may be different in different sections of the chorus from stage left to stage right, but should change gradually and uniformly and be determined ahead of time. All members should assume a strong yet relaxed posture and hold it throughout the performance. Singers in any chorus need to be reminded often about their posture.

Singers should never do anything with their eyes but look at the conductor, nor anything with their hands but hold the score. If long hair has been properly fastened and eyeglasses securely adjusted, there should be no need to use the hands for any other reason. When singing without music, hands may remain relaxed at the sides or clasped in front, but should be uniform throughout the chorus.

The conductor, possibly assisted by other observers, should correct any attention-getting behavior on the part of individual chorus members during rehearsals. Just one or two demonstrative singers can constitute a major distraction, changing the desired mood of the whole performance.

Figure 5.1.   A Single Distracted Chorus Member Can Affect the Audience's Concentration.

Music Folders

Singing from memory is always the preferable way to perform. The singers not only look more prepared but also can better concentrate on the conductor when they are not reading. At those times when printed music is necessary, carefully plan how it will look and how the singers will manage the music onstage.

Music should be held in folders of the same size, style, and color, arranged ahead of time in the order it will be performed. Everyone should be instructed to hold their music folders in the same hand and in the same uniform way in rest position as they walk out and before they get ready to sing. On cue from the conductor, they can practice opening the folders exactly together in the same way that they practiced synchronized standing and sitting.

Every singer should have his or her own folder so that each may adopt the same stance. It is difficult for singers to watch the conductor and to stand with good posture when sharing folders. The folders should be held at a height that allows the singers to glance at the music and also at the conductor by moving only their eyes, while their entire faces remain visible to the audience.

Acknowledging Applause

Plan and rehearse how the conductor and chorus will acknowledge applause together at the end of each piece as well as at the end of the concert. Decide whether the chorus will bow or simply remain standing during the applause. Practice the details of this part of the performance. If bowing, practice doing it exactly together on cue from the conductor. Whether bowing or not, the members of the chorus should remain standing, with good posture and pleasant facial expressions, folders held uniformly at their sides in rest position as the conductor is bowing, exiting, and reentering for additional bows. They should refrain from any conversation or wordless communication with their neighbors or with members of the audience.

Rehearse the bows of soloists and conductor as well as exits and reentrances for additional bows. Coordinate the dimming of the stage lights with the final exit of the conductor and soloists. Chorus members should remain standing still until the audience has completely stopped applauding, and then leave the stage in the same organized and rehearsed fashion in which they arrived at the beginning of the concert: holding folders uniformly, walking at a rehearsed, uniform pace, and not talking among themselves or looking at the audience.

After the Concert

Instruct singers on how to interact with audience members at the conclusion of the concert. They should accept praise graciously, without
contradicting listeners' opinions of the concert. It is unseemly and unprofessional to attempt to extract praise from audience members, to discuss
weaknesses in the concert, or to engage in conversations that are critical
of the conductor, soloists, or other chorus members or sections. Postconcert discussions with listeners should all be positive; the time for critical
evaluation among performers is at the next rehearsal.

TOTAL DISCIPLINE AND ORGANIZATION

Good stage presence in a large chorus requires thinking about dozens of
little details which may seem insignificant individually but, taken together, create a professional and organized appearance in which the audience may fully concentrate on the music. The demeanor of each and
every singer must blend in with all the others to avoid distraction. Dressing in a planned and coordinated fashion, rehearsing entrances, exits, and
bows, and establishing a detailed code of onstage deportment for the
singers all contribute to the final goal of creating a chorus that looks disciplined, poised, organized, and ready to sing.

LIST 5.1 DO'S AND DON'TS FOR CHORUS MEMBERS

Do

- Keep your concert attire clean, pressed, and in good condition.
- Keep your shoes polished and in good repair.
- Adjust eyeglasses so they will not ride down your nose.
- Practice your music so you do not need to be glued to the score.
- Bathe before dressing.
- Brush your teeth.
- Fasten and style your hair appropriately.
- Eat a light meal before the concert.
- Arrive early for the performance.
- Clear your head of personal problems.
- Arrange your music in the order you will sing it before going on-stage.
- Stand and sit still, with erect but not stiff posture.
- Concentrate on the music, whether singing or not.
- Keep your eyes on the conductor.
- Hold your music still.
- Maintain an appropriate and pleasant facial expression.
- Accept praise graciously.
- Keep postconcert conversations with the audience positive.

Don't

- Eat big meals before performing.
- Eat garlic or anything that may disagree with your stomach.
- Drink alcohol.
- Wear any perfumed products.
- Carry anything onstage but your music.
- Talk, gesture, or make eye contact with others while onstage.
- Move around when you sing.
- Take up too much room with your arms.
- Hold anything in your mouth.
- Touch your face or hair.
- Toss your hair.
- Beat time with your head or feet.
- Look around.
- Slump when sitting.
- Look overly enthusiastic, thus drawing attention to yourself.

(continued)

**LIST 5.1   DO'S AND DON'TS FOR
CHORUS MEMBERS (*continued*)**

- React to mistakes, your own or those of others.
- Mouth the words when others are singing.
- Applaud.
- Turn your back to the audience.
- Discuss weaknesses in the performance with audience members.
- Seek praise from audience members or ask their opinion of the concert.

Chapter 6

The Orchestra

An orchestra that does not watch the baton has no conductor.

—Hector Berlioz (1803–1869), composer, conductor

It is thrilling to see a disciplined orchestra (in this chapter, "orchestra" refers to any instrumental ensemble with a conductor) in which all players are obviously concentrating together as one under the conductor's baton. The appearance and demeanor of such a precision ensemble leads an audience to expect something wonderful and out of the ordinary, and they are rarely disappointed. The best orchestras look professional and poised down to the last member, from the time they come out onstage until the time they leave.

To achieve this high level of discipline and a uniform appearance, every orchestra not only needs a clear dress code and comprehensive onstage guidelines, but also standard procedures and personnel responsible for their enforcement.

RESPONSIBILITIES OF THE BOARD OF DIRECTORS, MANAGEMENT, AND CONDUCTOR

Whether actively aware of it or not, the leadership of any orchestra establishes the organization's standards on its stage presence. If you are part of such leadership—whether you are in charge of a student orchestra, an amateur orchestra, or a professional symphony—the stage presence of the ensemble is your responsibility. Collectively, you and your associates must decide exactly how you want your orchestra to look and act. Once you have established this, it is then necessary to set rules and provide the resources to make it happen. Regardless of how professional or experienced your players may be, they will be unable to project a unified image unless they have specific instructions particular to your organization.

To maximize the polished look of your ensemble, begin by establishing standards of dress and demeanor, stating them clearly in writing and distributing them to every member. No detail should be omitted from the written policy. This may seem fussy or excessive, but without spelling out exactly what you want—to the letter—you will not get the expected results.

You will probably be restricted by budgetary concerns, because good stage presence costs money in terms of time if not directly in cash. This is why the entire leadership of an orchestra, conductor, board of directors, and management must be involved in setting these standards. Wise leadership will realize, however, that the effect good stage presence can have on an audience is well worth the expense. Maintaining an organization whose poise and professionalism excites concertgoers will increase the size of the audience over time. This is truly the bread and butter of any performing organization. No matter how well they may actually play, it is difficult to keep an audience if your ensemble looks disorganized or if the players themselves do not appear engaged in the performances.

The Dress Code

A good dress code will ensure a coordinated and equally formal look among all the players. It will also prohibit elements of attire that may draw attention to individuals. The same principle that applies to solo performers applies as well to a large instrumental ensemble: the best concert attire does not compete with the music for the attention of the audience. This principle, of course, may be relaxed for less formal concerts in which the musicians dress for fun or for a comical effect.

Concert bands, modeled on military marching bands, traditionally wear dress military uniforms (or uniforms based on that model). Military dress codes are specific to the last detail (including even hairstyle and footwear), leaving no room for individuality of any kind. The result in the ensemble is the appearance of complete uniformity.

Orchestras, on the other hand, originated as entertainment for the nobility, performing in salons and ballrooms in livery dictated by the patron or even the building in which they performed—by the nineteenth century, in the stylish, formal dress clothing of the day. The custom of applying rigid military standards of uniformity to the orchestra's way of dressing has not survived in most orchestras, especially those with both male and female members.

Presently, ambiguities and generalities in most orchestra dress codes leave many details of the members' attire to individual choice. Orchestras need to be careful that their dress code or the enforcement of the dress code has not become so lax as to make the general appearance seem disorganized and visually chaotic. The heightened concentration and intensity that musicians want to project requires equivalent attention to attire. The amount of care that goes into dressing is a visual manifestation of the amount of care that went into preparing the music. Audiences find themselves unable to take a casually dressed orchestra nearly as seriously as they would if the players were dressed formally.

The Gender Issue

Added to the lack of specificity in orchestra dress codes is the complication brought about by the presence of both men and women in the group, since male and female formal attire has always been gender specific. Typically, although the appearance of uniformity is the goal, orchestra dress codes have different rules for men and women. When there are separate dress codes for each gender, the men's rules are relatively simple and compliance is relatively easy. This is because certain items of male dress, such as suits and tuxedos, hardly change style from year to year and are always readily available.

The women's rules, since women's fashions change every season and there is, as yet, no standard uniform for female orchestra members, usually allow for all sorts of outfits (dresses, pant suits, skirts and tops, slacks and tops, and so on). Experiments with formal attire have included permitting or requiring female members to dress in identical tuxedos as the men, and, at the other end of the spectrum, dispensing with the idea of uniformity altogether by having women dress in colorful ball gowns, as they might for any formal social function.

To achieve more uniformity, some orchestras have experimented with dressing the male and female players alike by having them dress in casual outfits: all in black pants and matching T-shirts, for example. The resulting look, although coordinated, can make the audience feel as if they are watching a rehearsal.

Still others have resorted to having an outfit custom made for their women players in a single style and material. This is the only way to have firm control over how the women in the orchestra look onstage. Although it may seem bothersome to get involved in design and dressmaking or tailoring, the trouble it will save on the performance end may be well worth it, by completely coordinating the women's clothing and eliminating visual disarray. The outfits may cost more, but the players will be saved the frustration of searching the department stores, where they cannot count on finding suitable solutions for items that will comply with the dress code. If yours is a professional orchestra, an authentic professional uniform is also a tax deduction.

In situations where the female members are expected to comply with a dress code on their own, they may have difficulty finding outfits in the required color (usually black or white). Complying with this seemingly simple color requirement is not so easy. There are many shades of black and many shades of white that, when mixed together under stage lights, do not contribute to a unified appearance within the ensemble. Stark white and various shades of cream do not look good together, for example. Black, too, comes in a variety of hues—especially when there are a variety of materials—that are visually incompatible.

Female players also need clothes that do not cling to the body and that do not leave too much flesh exposed. They must deal with the fact that women's fashions are usually created to be attention-getting, while the main point of an orchestra's dress code is that no single player stand out visually from the group. A strict dress code may also prohibit certain types of fabrics, such as velvet, satin, and open lace—even further limiting women's choices. Added to all these restrictions is the requirement that the outfit match the male tuxedo in level of formality. It is no wonder that among female players we see such a variety of outfits—often looking inappropriate—and that the visual impression given by an orchestra seems to deteriorate as the percentage of female players rises. This is a principal reason some conductors, whether they realize it or not, do not want women in their orchestras. It is no reflection on women as musicians, but rather a comment on our social customs regarding gender-specific dress. Developing a standard uniform for female players and making it consistently available to them is the only way this problem will be solved. When unable to provide your players with a uniform, it is helpful for them when dress codes are very specific, leaving as little as possible to individual choice.

Male Attire

A certain type of tuxedo, suit, or uniform should be required for men, specifying whether or not the coat has tails, whether to wear a cummerbund or waistcoat, the color and type of the tie, and the color of the cummerbund or waistcoat. It is best if fabrics are all exactly the same.

Female Attire

For women, it is important to prohibit certain fabrics that stand out under stage lighting, such as velvet, satin, and sequins or other sparkly material. Fabric should not be revealing (too sheer or lace too open). Hems of skirts and pants should be floor length, sleeves at least halfway between the elbow and wrist. Necklines should be modest both in front and in back. While bare arms, legs, and décolletage may be acceptable fashion, they make the female players look less serious and dignified than their male counterparts; furthermore, different amounts of exposed skin from person to person in the orchestra looks disorganized under the stage lights. All garments should drape in a flattering line without clinging to the body. If slim skirts or tight pants are worn, an overlaying garment should be required. In all cases, the women's attire should look as formal as—and no more formal than—the men's.

Jewelry and Hair

Flashy jewelry on the body or in the hair as well as dangling earrings or bracelets of any kind should be prohibited.

Great variety among hairstyles is another cause of visual disarray. Hairstyle is an important item in the dress code. Long hair hanging down looks incongruously informal when wearing dressy clothes. It must be fastened back, away from the face, requiring no adjustment during the concert. All hairstyles, including beards and mustaches, should be impeccably groomed to coordinate with formal dress.

Shoes and Hosiery

Shoes and hosiery are important, since much of the audience sits eye level with these. For both men and women there are all kinds of dress shoes, and it is best to require not simply black dress shoes but to specify a certain kind. Smooth leather, suede, and patent leather appear very different from each other and look disorderly when all are represented within the ensemble at the same time. Open toes, boots, and very high heels are not appropriate. The best presentation is for shoes to be completely uniform from member to member.

Hosiery must be black, not sparkly or otherwise highly decorated, long enough so that the tops are not seen (over the calf), and in a formal style consistent with the rest of the outfit. Like shoes, hosiery looks best when everyone is wearing exactly the same kind.

Alternate Dress Codes

Often, an orchestra will have more than one dress code for different performing situations. For example, there may be a less formal code for daytime concerts, or a lighter look for summer concerts. The guidelines should clearly prohibit the wearing of anything that would cause visual disarray in the ensemble or bring attention onto itself. Even for less formal concerts the dress code should be as specific as possible.

Size, Cleaning, and Maintenance

The dress code should stipulate that players are to wear clothes that fit well. It looks sloppy when some members are wearing clothes that are not the right size.

It is also important to require that concert clothing be regularly cleaned and pressed, and that the clothing not show wear of any kind. The audience can perceive dirty, worn, or wrinkled garments—to think otherwise is false.

Shoes, too, must be kept in pristine condition, not scuffed or worn. Hosiery must be free of runs.

Enforcement

The best dress code in the world is not worth much if it is not enforced, and good enforcement requires regular inspection. The services of a dressmaker or tailor can be used periodically to evaluate overall fit and condition of garments and to determine when they need to be replaced. It is good to appoint a staff member to conduct a preconcert inspection at every performance to cover all other matters. The dress code should outline penalties for various and repeated infractions. The inspector must apply these sanctions strictly, consistently, and fairly.

Frequently explain to the players the importance of the dress code for the success of the entire organization. You want them to become as interested as you are in having the orchestra look good onstage so that they are completely invested in the standards of your organization.

Onstage Guidelines

Orchestras usually perform on a stage without a curtain. This means that the audience may see and hear the players as they assemble before the performance and also at the end as they leave. It is important to consider how they all look and sound during these times as well as when they are actually performing.

Four Positions of Readiness

Members of the orchestra can practice assuming various postures together so that, at any given time, they may be in the same stage of readiness together as a group. There are four standard postures that instrumentalists typically learn: standing position, rest position, semi-rest position, and ready position.

The standing position is used when players walk out on a stage with an instrument and whenever the orchestra stands together to acknowledge applause. This usually happens when the conductor comes onstage at the beginning of the concert and again when the conductor calls for the players to stand during the applause at the end. Standing position itself is the appropriate way for the ensemble to acknowledge applause: musicians within the orchestra do not bow unless singled out individually.

In standing position, the players within the families of like instruments should hold their instruments (and their bows in the case of the string players) in the same formal way and at a uniform angle. Players should remain very still, never taking their eyes off the conductor. The row of musicians at the front of the orchestra, because they are closest to the audience, must pay particular attention to their appearance in standing position. It looks good if they face the audience when the full ensemble stands. The other players further to the back of the stage must be equally attentive to their standing position, however, if the disciplined appearance of the group as a whole is to be maintained.

Rest position is employed during long rests or during pieces or movements in which the instrument does not play at all. Instruments may be placed on the floor, on an instrument stand, or across the player's lap in rest position. Percussionists, harpists, and keyboard players may simply stand or sit quietly. Regardless of how long a musician must remain in rest position, his or her posture should not change—it should remain strong and upright with the head aligned and centered over the spine. The resting player should neither lean on the chair back nor slouch forward, and feet should remain on the floor. Throughout a long period of rest, the players' eyes should remain on the conductor while also following the score to be ready for the next entrance. When players relax their posture, are looking around, or are otherwise not paying attention, they distract the audience and weaken the concentration of everybody in the hall.

Figure 6.1.   Examples of Standing Position

Figure 6.2.   Examples of Full Rest Position

A semirest position is employed just before the conductor cues a ready position at the beginning of a piece, at the end of long rests just before playing again, and for short periods of rest in the music. From semirest position the players are able to assume the ready position at once.

In ready position, the players are holding their instruments up and are ready to play. They look as if they are about to do something, with all of their energy and concentration focused on the upcoming task. Erect and eager posture held slightly forward in a ready position creates the appearance of enthusiastic anticipation of the music to come. All eyes are on the conductor, waiting for a cue.

Musicians may have been taught slightly different ways to assume these positions. Most important is that each position is intentional and planned. Therefore, each orchestra needs to have its own standard definitions of the four positions and then to have the players practice them together until they look and feel precisely coordinated.

Before the Concert

All players should come onstage at the same time, just before the concert begins, so that the audience will not hear them practicing or see them doing the housework of setting up for the concert. All stage furnishings, scores, stands, and stationary instruments should have been set up and adjusted before the audience is allowed into the auditorium. The musicians should come onstage mentally ready for the performance, without talking among themselves or looking at the audience.

The players should carry an instrument or nothing at all. Other equipment necessary for the performance (secondary instruments, mutes, swabs, extra strings, music stand clips, and so on) should have been placed earlier at each playing position onstage. Leave all nonessential personal belongings (instrument cases, purses, sweaters, and so on) behind so they do not litter the stage. Carry instruments in a formal manner, and get quickly into formal rest position, sitting or standing, with good posture.

Warmups should have been done backstage, out of hearing of the audience, so that all members arrive onstage ready to tune when the concertmaster arrives. If there is a reason the orchestra members must warm up onstage, they should do so as quickly as possible. Appoint a member to be in charge of stopping the warmup before the entrance of the concertmaster, who should not have to enter while people are still playing.

The entrance of the concertmaster should be timed to happen as soon as all members have assumed their positions (or after the brief warmup). The lighting may change just at this point, with the lights onstage coming up

Figure 6.3.   Examples of Semirest Position

Figure 6.4. Examples of Ready Position

as the auditorium lights are dimmed. As the stage lights come up, all the players are sitting still and attentively waiting for the concertmaster. No stragglers should ever arrive onstage after this moment.

As the lighting changes, the audience will be drawn into the readiness and the silence of the players. The concertmaster then makes an entrance during this silence, goes to his or her position onstage, and bows to acknowledge applause. After the bow, the concertmaster will turn to direct the tuning of the orchestra section by section, in an organized fashion, as efficiently and quietly as possible, with players sounding only the usual tuning pitches.

The concertmaster will be seated at the conclusion of the tuning, making way for the entrance of the conductor. Someone backstage should be appointed to watch for the exact moment when the tuning has been completed and then to signal the conductor to go out onstage. It is anticlimactic if the conductor's entrance is delayed at the conclusion of the tuning.

All members should rise together upon the conductor's entrance, with the players in each section facing the same direction, holding their instruments in a uniform fashion. This move must be rehearsed to be precise and effective. One player who can see the conductor at the moment when he or she steps out onto the stage (this is not the concertmaster, who is usually facing in the other direction) may be appointed to cue the others to stand exactly together. For this to work well, all members must give their full concentration to the conductor's entrance—which, in turn, will generate excitement and anticipation among the audience.

The conductor enters and bows from the podium, so that he or she will not have to walk any distance after bowing, while the orchestra stands at attention. Then, facing the orchestra, the conductor gives the cue to be seated. The players then sit down exactly together, assuming the semirest position and then, on another cue, get into ready position. Orchestrating every detail of the conductor's entrance and the various positions of the players (standing, rest position, semirest position, and ready position) shows the audience that you are truly an ensemble—working, thinking, concentrating together—before you begin to play. A large group of people who are focused enough to move with precision in this way is exciting to watch. After such a carefully coordinated opening, the audience will await the first sound of the program with aroused anticipation.

At the Conclusion of the Concert

The conductor's bows and his or her invitation to the entire orchestra or to specific groups of players to stand and acknowledge applause should be rehearsed beforehand. When not standing to accept applause, all members remain in uniform rest position until the conductor has left the stage for the last time and the house lights come up. At this point, all of the players should leave the stage promptly, without conversation, carrying only their instruments. Cleaning and packing up instruments should be done backstage.

The Podium, Chairs, and Music Stands

Music stands should all have been set at a height from which players may see the printed music and also the conductor by moving only the eyes (not moving the whole head) and without craning the neck. The elevation of the conductor's podium depends on the height of the conductor: the taller the conductor, the lower the podium. Players closest to the conductor should not have to strain upward to see the conductor's face, hands, and baton; the players in back need a clear, unobstructed view.

Dented, dirty, worn out, and generally shabby stage furniture will be perceived by the audience. Although acquiring and maintaining good-looking stage furnishings is costly, an orchestra that wants to look its best cannot afford to overlook this significant aspect of its stage presence. Every performing organization needs a staff member to be in charge of the appearance of its stage furnishings.

THE RESPONSIBILITIES OF ORCHESTRA MEMBERS

First and foremost, faithfully adhere to your orchestra's published dress codes and stage guidelines. Take them seriously, and never try to bend the rules and thereby place stress on the entire organization.

If your ensemble warms up on the stage while there are audience members present, do so as quickly and quietly as possible. This is not the time to show off your upcoming solos or to demonstrate how high, fast, or loud you can play. Also, whether warming up backstage or onstage, it is extremely bad form to use portions of a guest artist's solo as warmup material (as if to show that you can play the piece too). When tuning with the orchestra, do so as quietly and quickly as you can, sounding only your tuning pitch.

Whenever you are onstage, remain in alert posture, without leaning on your chair back or slouching forward, and keep your feet under you. Try to appear mentally awake and involved in what is going on even between pieces. Be actively involved with seemingly passive activities, such as waiting for the conductor, listening during rests, and sitting while the audience applauds. Never allow yourself to look disinterested, bored, or tired. Be careful not to adopt a trancelike stare during those times when you are not playing. Leave your watch backstage.

Figure 6.5. Poor Posture Conveys Disinterest in the Performance and Lack of Discipline in the Ensemble.

Do not converse or engage in any type of wordless communication that is not directly relevant to the performance. Refrain from reacting with your facial expression to mistakes or to any out-of-the-ordinary occurrence onstage. Similarly, save your expressions of approval for others' playing for after the concert. Do not look at the audience or turn around to look at anything behind you (another player, the chorus, a film). Never take your eyes off the conductor when you are playing as well as when you are not. Know your music well enough so you do not need to read it note for note.

While performing, keep body movement to a minimum. Do not violate the personal space of the players around you. Refrain from beating time with any part of your body or swaying back and forth or in circles. Keep your legs still and arms, legs, and feet close to the body. Do not draw attention to yourself with demonstrative enthusiasm. Instead, develop a look of intense, still concentration as you play.

Turn your pages gently, without disturbing the air around you. If you are responsible for page turning, always be prepared with clips to fasten the score to the stand if necessary. If you have equipment that must be set on the floor—a mute, for example—place a cloth under it to eliminate the possibility of making noise when putting it down during the concert. Refrain from cleaning your instrument or turning pages during someone's solo.

In the event of a musical emergency, when an instrument has a mechanical failure, it is appropriate for a musician in a lesser position immediately to give over his or her instrument to the soloist, first chair, or more highly ranked player.

Attend to every detail of your attire as stipulated in the orchestra's dress code. Wear clothing that fits you perfectly, changing it whenever your body size changes. Choose footwear and hosiery that goes with the rest of your outfit and conforms to the dress code. If your hair is long enough to fall into your face, make sure it is well groomed and fastened back securely. Do not wear anything on your fingers (with the possible exception of a wedding ring) or wrists or paint your nails. If you wear glasses, make sure they fit snugly and will not ride down your nose.

Eliminate the possibility of having body odor by bathing just before the concert. Clean and press your concert attire regularly. Do not wear perfumed products of any kind to rehearsals or concerts.

Never chew gum or hold anything in your mouth. Do not bring reading material of any kind onstage during concerts or rehearsals.

Arrive early and stay late. It is rude to come onstage after the conductor has arrived or to leave while the conductor is still there.

THE PIT ORCHESTRA

Some think that the pit orchestra need not be so concerned with issues of stage presence, since they are sitting down in the pit away from the view of the audience. However, the overall discipline of a performing organization is just as important when the audience cannot see you. Good posture, uniform dress, attention to the conductor, the appearance of being totally engaged in the performance—all of these elements have an effect on the musicians themselves, and help to create the best performance an organization can produce.

Also, it is an unusual situation when the pit orchestra is not visible from loges and balconies. People sitting in those sections are part of the audience as well, and there is enough illumination from music stands for them to see clearly whether the musicians are truly involved in the performance or not. The pit orchestras of some of the best professional opera companies often act as if this portion of the audience is not even there. Especially distracting is the practice of allowing musicians to come in and out in the middle of an act to avoid sitting for long periods of time while not playing. This cannot help but break the concentration of the conductor, other musicians, and a significant portion of the audience repeatedly throughout a long performance.

Possibly the most serious infraction is for the players to pack up and leave at the end of a performance as soon as their last note is played, while the audience is applauding. This is rude and inconsiderate to the conductor, the singers, and the audience and gives a bad impression of the organization as a whole. As with onstage orchestras, members of the pit orchestra should remain present as long as the conductor is there.

OBSTACLES TO GOOD STAGE PRESENCE

The financial realities of maintaining a professional orchestra sometimes force, or at least encourage, an organization to cut corners in matters of their stage presence. For example, poorly paid pit orchestra players may, in the absence of a deserved pay raise, be given the privilege of leaving as soon as their part in the performance is over. Perhaps the management, not wanting to have to pay the musicians for the extra time, will actually require them to leave.

Morale among professional orchestra members can be a problem. As wonderful as any orchestra concert is, players who perform in the same ensemble week in and week out can easily become stale and worn down by the routine of their job. It takes strong leadership to keep players fully invested in the success of the organization so that they can put 100 percent of themselves into each performance. Because poor morale, although intangible, is obvious and demoralizing to an audience, the leadership of large performing groups should go to any lengths necessary to keep their players' enthusiasm high.

A professional or an amateur orchestra that has a good dress code and stage guidelines may still look bad onstage because it cannot afford the time or the money it takes to enforce the rules consistently. There may be inadequate funds to maintain the scores in good condition and to replace them when necessary. The stage furnishings may get shabby, with no money to buy new ones.

Most conductors feel that there is always too little rehearsal time, and naturally they want to use every bit of this time preparing the music for performance rather than rehearsing entrances, exits, and bows, for example. Attending to details of stage presence can seem to be an unattainable luxury.

OVERCOMING THE OBSTACLES

There are personnel in any large orchestra who would enjoy the job of improving and maintaining the group's visual presentation and who would take on the task of raising funds to accomplish this. Finding these people and setting them to work takes nothing more than the leadership's interest in making this happen. When the board members, management, and conductor become fully aware of the importance of stage presence and when they realize that poor stage presence can seriously curtail the overall success of their organization, it will become a priority. Good stage presence comes at a high cost. The return on the investment will be great, however, measured by the effect it will have on your audience. In this sense, no orchestra can afford to be without it..

LIST 6.1   THINGS YOUR CONDUCTOR SHOULD NEVER HAVE TO SAY

- Watch me.
- Stop talking (gesturing, winking, rolling your eyes, flirting, giggling).
- Wake up.
- Get rid of the gum.
- Put down the magazine (book, newspaper, letter).
- Stop fidgeting during the solo.
- Clean your tuxedo.
- Turn your pages quietly.
- Don't wear that cologne (hair spray, aftershave).
- Stop tapping your foot (bobbing your head, moving around).
- Relax your face.
- Take a bath (use mouthwash).
- Sit up straight.
- Leave your belongings (purses, sweaters, instrument cases) backstage.
- Be onstage before I arrive and do not leave until I go.

Music directors of amateur and student ensembles may often be heard saying these things. In a professional context, however, conductors are sometimes reluctant to insult the intelligence and experience of their musicians by pointing out such basic transgressions. It is presumed that professional players know better even though their behavior may not always show it. It is the responsibility of every ensemble member to take care of these things in the context of both rehearsals and performances, and every orchestra needs to have a procedure in place to correct infractions.

Chapter 7

The Conductor as Leader

The real end and aim of a conductor should be, in my opinion, that his presence should be apparently unnecessary. His place is at the helm, and not at the oars.

—Franz Liszt (1811–1886), composer and pianist

Conductors provide much of the legendary material of music history. The great conductors have been imposing figures who, by sheer force of their personalities and their exceptional musicianship, maintain authoritarian command over dozens, sometimes even hundreds, of musicians. A good conductor will use his or her charisma to focus the concentration of the players and audience alike on every note of the work being performed, keeping the excitement high from the first note to the last. Good stage presence, an indispensable element in the conductor's overall presentation, helps accomplish this.

Most performing organizations have a hierarchy of leadership that usually includes many people, the conductor (or music director) being only one of these. As a conductor, therefore, you will never be given the authority to make all the decisions. In addition to purely musical duties, you will find yourself involved in the politics of keeping budgets balanced, maintaining personnel satisfaction, and dealing with board members, faculties, and/or management. You may have minimal stated authority.

Regardless of how much power you are actually given by the policies of the organization, however, everyone will look to you as the moral and artistic leader of the group, the person who sets and enforces the standards, who demands discipline, who is uncompromising in musical matters. And, in fact, the best conductors *are* such people, those who can push others to heights they would not otherwise attain, often with nothing more than their own steadfast ideals.

Since budgetary matters are involved, it is preferable that there be an organizationwide policy, and funds designated for the establishment and maintenance of the organization's stage presence. Even with such a policy, however, the actual day-to-day stage presence of your chorus or orchestra largely depends on your own rules and your ability to enforce them. You will do this by commanding the respect of the musicians, maintaining high morale among them, and exercising a strong power of persuasion among your colleagues.

COMMAND RESPECT AND REQUIRE CONCENTRATION

Audiences are impressed when the members of a performing organization are respectful toward their conductor. This show of respect draws them into the performance before it begins, as soon as you appear on stage. Therefore, it is important to require that your ensemble respond immediately to your entrance by standing exactly together as you come onstage at the outset of a concert. Practice getting all members in various stages of readiness: standing, rest, semirest, and ready positions. Ultimately, you want the ensemble to react instantly to your cues. This means that they will be ready and waiting for your direction at all times. You should never have to do anything demonstrative to get their attention.

MOVE AS LITTLE AS POSSIBLE

Conductors must give unmistakable and suggestive signals to the orchestra, not choreography to the audience.

—George Szell (1897–1970), conductor

You look most powerful and effective when your cues to the ensemble are subtle. This is true when actually conducting the music as well as when cueing readiness positions. If your direction is grandiose, or if it looks as if you are working too hard to get the musicians to follow you, your influence over them will appear weaker than if you can achieve the desired results with small and apparently effortless motions. A minimum of movement on your part is also less distracting for the audience.

CONDUCT WITH GOOD POSTURE

Good posture is a characteristic of most successful leaders. To project your image as the ensemble's capable and effective conductor, carry yourself well. Keep a strong back, and hold your head on top of your spine, always looking out in front of you. Hold your shoulders down and back and keep your arms and hands natural and relaxed. Be conscious of being able to breathe deeply, with an open chest and head up at all times.

When using the score, place the music stand so that you may see the music without bending your head forward. Do not let your eyes become glued to the score throughout the performance, and do not let the use of the score negatively affect your good, strong posture. Turn pages as unobtrusively as possible. It is best when the audience is unaware that there is music in front of you.

DRESS FOR THE JOB

When conducting, you need to be able to use a full range of motion in your arms. Whatever you wear should not impede this movement, nor should your clothes look stressed as you conduct. This requires special attention, because dress clothes are not usually constructed to allow for large arm movements, and may burst at the seams or pucker unattractively unless tailored with this need in mind.

Figure 7.1. When Not Tailored to Accommodate Required Body Movement, Clothing Will Look Stressed.

Hems of skirts and trousers should not rise and fall with your arm movement. Pay attention to the appearance of your footwear, assuming that it will be eye level with a good portion of your audience, and make sure your shoes provide enough support so you may stand throughout the concert without undue fatigue. Wear clothing at least as formal as the full ensemble's attire.

Keep your hair short or fasten it back away from your face. It is distracting for the musicians, for the audience, and most important for *you* if you have to repeatedly push hair out of your eyes during a performance. Do not wear anything on your fingers or wrists.

Evaluate Your Appearance from Behind

A conductor is usually the only musician who performs with his or her back to the audience. (Organists also play with their backs to the audience, but often they are out of sight altogether. When playing within sight of the audience, this consideration is important for organists as well.) It is difficult to imagine how you appear from behind without viewing a video recording of yourself. Weak posture is especially noticeable from this vantage point. If you have a habit of bending forward at the waist as you conduct, you will see that this projects your derrière into an unflattering position in some clothing—especially when viewed from below, where much of the audience will be sitting. This is one reason conductors traditionally wear tails or long jackets. Avoid any clothing that clings to the body.

GENEROUSLY SHARE ACCOLADES WITH OTHER MUSICIANS

As the conductor, you may be the leader of the ensemble, but this does not mean that you accept all the credit for its accomplishments. Without the musicians under your baton there would be no performance. Audiences are attracted to conductors who are, in addition to being firm disciplinarians, generous in their public appreciation of the other musicians in the organization.

Acknowledge the contributions of individual singers, players, or sections during the applause. Although you may want this to appear spontaneous, it is best to plan and rehearse it ahead of time. Decide exactly what will happen during the final applause: which individuals or sections will be asked to stand, the order in which they will be asked, how long each will remain standing, what the cue is to be seated, and so forth— always planning that all curtain calls will cease when the applause begins to wane.

PRECISELY TIME ENTRANCES AND EXITS

Coordinate all entrances and exits with your stage manager. There should not be an anticlimactic wait for your entrance at the outset of the concert. Make sure that either you or the concertmaster enter as soon as the house lights go down, the stage lights come up, and the audience gets quiet. Time your entrance similarly with the lighting after an intermission. If the concertmaster is the first to enter for the purpose of tuning, enter promptly at the end of the tuning, at the moment the concertmaster is being seated.

Before intermissions and at the end of the concert, it should be obvious to the audience when you have stopped coming back for bows by having the house lights up and the stage lights dimmed as you exit for the last time.

Guest Soloists

When there is a guest soloist or soloists, entrances, bows, and exits with the conductor also need rehearsal if they are to look polished. As the conductor, it is your responsibility to orchestrate these moves, and to adapt the customs of your organization to the style of the visiting soloist(s). Generally, the conductor follows the soloist(s) both on and off the stage. When coming on, the soloist goes to the place where he or she will perform, and the conductor passes behind the soloist and goes directly to the podium. At this point, the soloist takes a bow while the conductor also faces front, either bowing together with the soloist or just watching, but allowing the focus to be on the soloist during the initial bow. Because details can vary, they should always be rehearsed. The guest performer will appreciate the time you take to do this.

At the end of the performance, any number of things may happen. The soloist may embrace the conductor, or shake the hand of both conductor and concertmaster, before doing a solo bow. Then the conductor and soloist may bow together. The conductor may want the orchestra or certain sections of the ensemble to stand to accept their own applause. It is inappropriate for a soloist to bow while the audience is clapping for the orchestra. In the case of multiple soloists, it is important to decide who will lead the group on and off the stage and the order in which they will walk. The conductor can plan all these moves so that nothing looks awkward or clumsy during the applause.

CONSCIOUSLY PLAN YOUR ENSEMBLE'S PRESENTATION

As a conductor, you are responsible for the stage presence of many people at once. You are the person on whom the entire organization relies for standards, guidance, and enforcement. You must think about all the details, lay plans, hold rehearsals, and be able to convince management of the importance of your overall presentation. This is a dimension of your job that will almost certainly contribute to a major goal of your entire organization: the growth and retention of your audience.

Chapter 8

On the Day of the Concert

Three qualities are essential in a professional musician . . . the first is good health and the other two are the same.

—Mark Hambourg (1879–1961), pianist

An important and sometimes overlooked aspect of stage presence is the general well-being of the performer(s). You need to be feeling well to look your best, and you cannot be feeling rushed and frantic if you are to take care of all the important details of your concert in addition to playing well.

Whether performing frequently or only once or twice a year, to be successful you must learn to take care of your health, get enough rest, eat well, practice sufficiently, conduct rehearsals, and have adequate time for bathing, dressing, grooming, and checking out the conditions in the concert hall. It takes careful planning to make time for all these things while also keeping yourself as calm and focused as possible before your concert.

PERSONAL NEEDS

First, determine your optimum schedule on the day of a concert. When do you like to get up? How long will you practice and where? When will rehearsals be scheduled? How much time would you like to have in the hall? Are you meeting with a piano tuner and, if so, when and for how long? Do you need meetings with the stage personnel, or with a page turner? When would you like to eat? What would you like to eat? Do you need time to rest, and if so, when, where, and for how long? How much time do you need for bathing, dressing, and getting ready? How long before the beginning of the concert would you like to arrive at the hall? What are your needs backstage during the concert and immediately following the performance? Once you know the answers to these and all similar questions, you can arrange your day, leaving plenty of time for everything you need to do. It is helpful to develop your own personal checklist and routine schedule for days on which you will perform.

HOSTS, PATRONS, AND FANS

If you are not completely in charge of your schedule on concert day—if you are in another city, for example—you must make your needs known to the people around you. You may fear being regarded as a prima donna if you make too many demands on people who may not understand the importance of some of your requests. Sometimes this cannot be helped. It is better to be seen as a finicky person than a bad performer, and often this is exactly the choice you must make. More experienced performers learn how to make their needs known. If you are young and less experienced, people can take advantage of you before you learn to express your needs clearly and completely.

Some hosts, especially less experienced ones, will be relieved if you tell them exactly what you want to do throughout the day of a concert, because they may be under the mistaken impression that you need to be entertained. If you fill the whole day with your requested schedule, they will see that they do not have to worry about keeping you occupied.

It is also in your interest as a performer to build good relationships with your hosts, patrons, and fans, who will want to have personal contact with you of one sort or another. On the day of your concert you may be invited to attend a dinner or a reception. You may also be asked to sign autographs or copies of your recordings. Some hosts will want you to help promote your concert by being interviewed in the media.

The best way to juggle the wishes of your hosts and your personal necessities is to spell out your most important needs in writing, well before the concert, and to ask your host to honor them. This will eliminate last minute surprises, because you will be consulted if your host wants to make any changes in your stipulated schedule, and you will be able to make decisions case by case. When unfamiliar with your surroundings, do not forget to inquire about the length of time it takes to get to a proposed activity and to return afterward.

Ask that your hotel be close to the concert hall, or at least that you can remain close to the hall all day before the concert. Driving around in traffic can be very stressful, and you will encounter hosts who are bad drivers. You will not be able to return to your room to bathe and dress before the concert if the hotel is too far from the hall.

Spell out your meal requests, including preferred menus and times. Do not be persuaded to go to restaurants that are too far from the hall on the day of the concert. Decline preconcert social dinner engagements. Let your hosts know ahead of time if you want something to eat and drink in your dressing room and if there is anything else you may need to have backstage during the concert.

Ask that no well-wishers visit your dressing room before the concert or during intermission. Afterward, you can put limits on how long you will greet the public or how long you will sign autographs. If you look forward to the postconcert reception, you may want to stay until the end, but if you do not enjoy parties, limit the time you are willing to remain at such events. Request something to eat and drink before meeting people at a reception. Too often, performers are not offered anything before being placed in a receiving line or being asked to sign autographs. Reception food is often not adequate in any case. If you need a good meal after the concert, request one, and plan to arrive late at the reception.

Learn to Decline Requests

Applause is a receipt, not a bill.

—Artur Schnabel (1882–1951), pianist,
explaining his refusal to play encores

At the end of a concert, do not perform encores if you are tired and feel you cannot do your best. Also, it is in bad taste for your hosts to request informal performances at other times, and therefore always appropriate to decline such requests. Practice gracious ways to escape overly zealous or long-winded fans. If you play an instrument, avoid prolonged hand shaking or autograph signing, as both activities can stress your hand.

Avoid Awkward Situations

Being clear about your needs before the concert will save you from such awkward situations as: having to decline a preconcert dinner party at the last minute, having to cancel sightseeing plans, or having to ask a delegation of VIP patrons to leave your dressing room during intermission. Most hosts are happy to help carry out your wishes if they know what they are, and will understand that certain things must be important to you when you have gone to the trouble of enumerating them ahead of time.

PROTECT YOUR WELL-BEING

Performing music is a very demanding job, more demanding than non-performers usually realize. Therefore, do not expect that others, even those accustomed to working with professional musicians, will anticipate your individual needs on the day of a concert. It is up to you to express your needs very clearly and well ahead of time to the people who can help you schedule the day as you need it to be.

Every day, do your best to maintain your health by eating well, getting enough rest, minimizing stress, and avoiding unhealthy habits. There is a significant athletic component to being a performing musician, and you, just like any athlete, will perform best when in peak condition.

LIST 8.1   THINGS TO DO ON CONCERT DAY

Go over your personal checklist(s) early in the day (after having already reviewed them earlier in the week), to make sure all is ready and in order.

- Outline your schedule in detail.
- Review tasks with the stage manager and other helpers.
- Make time for adequate rest, practice, and preferred relaxation routines.
- Eat well, avoiding sugar, caffeine, alcohol, and anything that might upset your stomach.
- Decline social engagements before the concert and during intermission.
- Visualize an exciting, enjoyable performing experience.

Chapter 9

The Stage and Its Furnishings

Hints to those who have pianofortes: Keep your piano free from dust, and do not allow needles, pins, or bread to be placed upon it, especially if the key-board is exposed, as such articles are apt to get inside and produce a jarring or whizzing sound.

—*Enquire Within upon Everything*, 1860

The stage upon which you perform, as well as the furniture and the piano you use are important aspects of your presentation that should not be overlooked. Consider the stage a special place, the visual context for your concert. Avoid performing in any venue that you cannot visit beforehand, so that there will be time to make requests of the stage manager. As with all other aspects of stage presence, follow the principle that you want a distraction-free environment in which your audience can concentrate on the music.

MAKE THE STAGE CLEAN AND UNCLUTTERED

Performers frequently play in halls over which they have no control. Consequently, if the stage is in generally poor condition, needing paint or repairs, there is little you can do about this—except possibly to play in a different hall.

Regardless of its overall condition, however, the stage itself, as well as any permanent equipment that you may be using, such as a piano, podium, or risers, should be clean. Request that cleaning be done before the concert or, when there is no staff at your disposal, do it yourself.

Make sure the stage is not littered with nonessential objects such as chairs, music stands, risers, podiums, instruments, or anything else that you will not be using in your concert. Request that the stage be emptied of all such items or move them backstage yourself.

Your chairs and stands look best when they are uniform in style and color, clean, and in good condition without dust, fingerprints, scratches, or dents. Take care of this equipment as you would your instrument. Stands should have a solid backing and be large enough to hide the widest and highest score you will use. It is safest to bring your own chairs and stands with you unless you know ahead of time that the hall will be well equipped for your performance.

PLACEMENT

In general, performers should be centered on the stage. This means that a conductor will be standing at the exact center, and a chamber group will be clustered about the center. The keyboard of a piano will be lined up along the center perpendicular line for a solo performance and about two feet to the left of this line (as viewed from the audience) when performing with a soloist. Do not position the piano at an angle.

Once you have determined the center of the stage from left to right, you must decide how far back on the stage you and any other performers should be positioned. Take into consideration the acoustics of the hall, sight lines from the audience, and, if necessary, the lighting. There will be one spot from which sound will project the best into the hall. Experienced performers can find this place even without the presence of the audience. There are times when problems with lighting will force you to move to a

Figure 9.1.   A Cluttered Stage Is an Inappropriate Setting for a Concert.

less acoustically desirable place on the stage. This is a very unfortunate situation. The best stages have lighting that can adapt to the position you have chosen based solely on musical considerations.

LIGHTING

Before the concert, decide on the settings for both the stage lighting and the lighting in the house. You will want the stage lighting to come up and the house lights to dim just before the performers walk onstage, and for the reverse to happen just before intermission and at the end of the concert after the final bow.

Direct spotlights to center stage if there will be only one performer. As the size of the ensemble increases, strong lighting should illuminate more of the stage. As much as possible, eliminate any distracting shadows or any glaring lights that will blind the musicians. It may be necessary to use lighting on individual music stands, so be prepared with this equipment. To remove all shadows from the keyboard, pianists ideally require lighting from directly above, but unfortunately this is often not available. Always rehearse with the lighting that will be used at the concert.

Ask the lighting engineer to coordinate the changes in stage and house lighting with the ushering staff, so that latecomers do not disrupt the dramatic entrance of the musicians onstage, their concentrated preparation, and the first sounds of the concert.

FLOWERS

The atmosphere of a concert can be enhanced when the stage is dressed up with flowers. If you have a single bouquet, its size should be in proportion to the size of the stage and the hall. It is better to have no flowers than to have an arrangement that looks too small. Numerous smaller plants or bunches of cut flowers may be used to line the lip of the stage. Get the advice of a florist or decorator if you want flowers but feel that you cannot make the best choices regarding size, type, and stage placement. Flowers should tastefully enhance the overall picture that the performers wish to present, and not look out of place or overwhelm the stage.

THE PIANO PROBLEM

Musical instruments are beautiful, aesthetic objects, and most musicians take pride in keeping their own instruments looking as good as possible by cleaning and packing them away after every time they play. Pianists (some aspects of this discussion apply as well to percussionists and players of all other keyboard instruments), however, are rarely tutored in procedures of instrument care. There are a number of reasons for this. First, a technician is usually relied upon to care for the instrument. Since frequent tuning is important as well as expensive, it is easy for the pianist to feel as if the piano is being well maintained simply by calling the technician. Second, pianists almost always perform on instruments they do not own. Thus, it may seem unimportant to care for the appearance of one's own piano, since the audience will never see it. Third, the case of a grand piano is something that can seem more like a piece of furniture than a musical instrument because it gathers dust and, when the lid is down, provides a large surface upon which it is tempting to place things. Fourth, as with a piece of fine furniture, it takes time and money to keep the piano looking in pristine condition.

It is not uncommon, then, that the appearance of musicians' personal pianos deteriorates after a few years, with an accumulation of fingerprints and dirt on the case and keys and dust piling up under the strings. Dents and scratches caused by using the instrument as a table, by bumping into it with other objects, or by moving it, go unrepaired. The interior of the instrument is usually not cleaned by the average technician.

Pianos not personally owned by individual musicians—those in schools, conservatories, and concert halls—fare even worse. Typically, the piano may be tuned regularly and have occasional adjustments and repairs that affect the way the instrument sounds and the way it responds to the performer, but very rarely will an organization provide for maintaining the appearance of even their best piano. No pressure is brought to bear by the people playing the piano either, because visiting pianists will typically take an interest only in the condition and the tuning of the instrument, just as they do at home.

Employees of the institution that owns the piano and other musicians have no pride of personal ownership, and they are rarely instructed in the care and maintenance of the piano's appearance. When not in use, the piano serves as a tabletop. When it is being moved about onstage, you may see the piano being bumped into things or serving as a dolly for the piano bench or other items. Typically, none of the people around the piano treat it as the magnificent instrument that it is.

From the standpoint of good stage presence, a piano on a stage should look like a new piano in a showroom. Only in this condition will the appearance of the instrument be congruent with the other formalities observed by the performer(s). Dirt, fingerprints, scratches, and dents are all visible to the audience. A pianist in a formal gown or tuxedo sitting at an abused piano paints a very incongruous picture. As the performer, you may want the piano in the hall to look better, but if it has suffered years of neglect there is not too much you can do in the last hours before a concert.

Until caring for the instrument becomes a routine aspect of piano pedagogy and awareness of the impression made by the piano's appearance is raised among all musicians, the "piano problem" will not go away.

Moving the Piano during a Concert

Whenever there is occasion for the piano to be moved on and off the stage during a concert, it is important that it be treated as a musical instrument. The protective, padded cover should be removed backstage before the piano is brought out. If the cover has any metal parts, such as grommets or buckles, take care not to scratch the piano with them. No items should ever be transported on the piano lid. Stagehands who move the piano should be dressed up and not look like furniture movers. They can keep the shiny surface of the piano free of fingerprints by wearing gloves or by wiping any new fingerprints from the case with a soft cloth carried expressly for this purpose. With practice, the job can be done expertly and efficiently, minimizing the time the audience must wait between pieces.

Other musicians who may need to move their chairs and stands to make way for the piano or for any other kind of onstage rearrangement should know exactly where they are going and move there promptly and quietly, without conversation and without turning their backs to the audience. It is good to rehearse these moves so they take up as little time as possible during the concert.

STAGE PRESENCE INCLUDES THE STAGE, ITS FURNITURE, AND INSTRUMENTS

It is a pity if, after rehearsing your music, choosing just the right attire, and studying all aspects of your comportment on stage, the concert takes place in shoddy surroundings. First and foremost, make sure the stage and its furnishings are clean. Request that the piano be cleaned and polished, or do it yourself. Use uniform chairs and stands and keep them free of obvious dents and scratches.

All musicians, not just pianists, should be aware of the importance of treating pianos, and other instruments that are the property of the hall or the organization, as the fine instruments they are, and should devote time and energy to their care. Too often it is the piano or other shared instruments that undermine the effort you have put into other areas of your stage presence.

Chapter 10

Nonperforming Personnel

In the opera house . . . you depend even on the man who operates the curtain. If he lets it down or up too early or too late, at a stroke he ruins a pianissimo!

—Karl Böhm (1894–1981), conductor

If you perform in the same hall all the time, or if your organization is large enough to have its own support staff, you have the luxury of having the time to familiarize your helpers with your ongoing needs and to train them in all the details. It is often the case, however, when musicians perform in various venues, that they must work with people they do not know well or at all. In these cases, it is important to consider what kinds of needs should be communicated before your performance and to whom your requests should be directed.

Every performing venue has a staff of one or more people whose job it is to provide assistance to the performers and to see that concerts run smoothly. Staff members can best do this when performers communicate their needs in a clear and organized fashion and when they are asked to participate in problem solving.

Do not assume that nonperforming personnel, no matter how experienced and professional they may be, will anticipate all your needs. You, the performer, are responsible for making all of your requests known to the staff well ahead of time. You must therefore plan the time to make this important communication.

TYPICAL POSITIONS

Not all venues have a full-time staff member performing each of these functions, and some venues have more than one. The following list of positions represents tasks that must be done behind the scenes of any performance. Performers should not have to do anything but perform on the day of a concert, and they should certainly not do any housekeeping tasks in front of the audience. Therefore, whenever the venue does not provide the personnel, others should be appointed to carry out this essential work.

Concert Manager

The concert manager is in charge of booking the hall. When first communicating with the concert manager about the date of your concert, make sure you include all the times at which your performance will have an impact on the venue. For example, if you will have equipment delivered, let the concert manager know exactly when it will be delivered and by whom. Provide the name and phone number of the movers. Ask for the name and number of the person to whom the movers should report. Make sure to find out where the equipment will be stored before your rehearsal and concert and who is responsible for moving it to the stage before you perform.

If you need to have a piano tuned, ask for the tuner's name and number and find out the schedule of the tuning. If you will schedule your own tuner, find out the times when the piano may be tuned and give the concert manager the tuner's name, phone number, and tuning schedule.

Make sure to give the concert manager an estimate of the time you need for rehearsal in the hall. Ask the name of the person who will be there to let you in, and find out how to contact that person in the event the building is closed when you get there. If possible, meet him or her beforehand. Ask about security measures during rehearsals, and what procedure to follow to exit and reenter the building.

In estimating the ending time for your concert, it is best to say that the concert will end later than it actually will, allowing the stage personnel to be finished earlier than planned or, at least, on time. Do not forget to add the time it will take for you to pack up your things and for the audience to leave.

Finally, tell the concert manager when your equipment will be moved from the hall. Get the name and number of the person to whom the movers should report, and make sure the movers have the appropriate information.

Stage Manager

The stage manager will set up the stage before your event and make any desired changes on the stage during the concert. He or she also can control the temperature of the hall and will supervise the lighting, both on the stage and in the auditorium. Stage managers and their helpers, the stagehands, are there to help make your performance run smoothly. It is in your best interest to utilize their expertise as much as possible, but this requires communicating detailed instructions to them and, in some cases, holding rehearsals.

Early on, make the request that the stage be cleaned and cleared of all unnecessary items. If your concert will use the piano, ask that the case of the instrument and the legs of the bench be polished.

Make sure you tell the stage manager exactly where you want every piece of equipment—risers, stands, chairs, podium, instruments, and so forth—positioned on the stage. If a musician has adjusted his or her equipment beforehand—for example, setting the height of the piano bench or the tilt and height of the music stand—request that these adjustments be carefully maintained.

Clearly describe all changes in the stage setup that will happen during the concert and exactly when they will happen. If there are more than one or two simple changes, outline them all in writing. It is helpful for the stagehands if you mark the stage floor with tape—a separate color for each change—to show where everything should be. Ask the stagehands to make these changes in a specific way—that they carry single items in an upright position with both hands, for example, and that they do not turn their backs to the audience.

Request that any person who will come onstage during the concert be dressed appropriately. If the stagehands in that venue are not accustomed to dressing for performances, you may want to appoint your own helpers to do this onstage work, but performers should refrain from doing it themselves.

It is a good idea to give the stage manager or supervising stagehand a generous tip *before* your performance, thanking him or her for all the anticipated help that will make your concert a success.

Lighting Engineer

The stage manager may be in charge of the lighting, but there may also be a lighting engineer. In either case, check out the stage lighting beforehand to see that the lighting appropriately highlights the important places on the stage. Ask the lighting engineer to adjust the lighting to your needs, and do not position yourself or your equipment to adapt to the lighting unless it cannot be adjusted. Make sure the lighting illuminates your face as you bow, and be careful that it does not cast annoying shadows on piano keys or shine too strongly in your eyes as you play. Make sure all the musicians can see their music. Sometimes separate illumination may be required on individual music stands.

Plan the lighting before, during, and after the concert, deciding how much to dim the auditorium during the performance and how much to dim the stage before and after. Coordinate the changing of the stage and auditorium lighting with your entrance and with your final bows. Musicians should enter promptly after the stage lights come up at the beginning of a concert, and auditorium lights should come up immediately after the performers have left the stage for the last time. Lapses in the timing at these crucial junctures create anticlimactic moments that are best avoided.

Audio/Visual Engineer

If you will need audiovisual equipment during the concert, or simply a microphone to make announcements before the concert, make these needs known ahead of time so that a person who has experience with the equipment will have time to set it up for you. Always rehearse the use of such apparatus. This spares your audience the frustration of waiting while you make last minute adjustments or while you figure out how to work the equipment. It is also important to protect everyone's ears from the shriek of a poorly adjusted microphone.

It has become necessary to remind audiences before a concert to turn off electronic devices that may make noise: cell phones, pagers, watches, and so forth. A live, verbal announcement for this purpose is more effective than a written reminder in a program. This announcement may come from backstage over the sound system or by an onstage announcer, but do not forget to request sound equipment for this short speech.

Stagehands should remove all audiovisual equipment from the stage as soon as you are finished with it.

Ushers

Some performers may think of ushers as having nothing to do with the concert itself, but they can play a key role in the overall stage presentation. If you have gone to the trouble of carefully orchestrating your entrance, of bringing the audience into your concentration, and of building up a feeling of anticipation and excitement, you want to make sure that nothing disturbs the critical moments before you begin to play or sing.

You can rely on the ushers to keep latecomers from interfering with the intense atmosphere you have tried so hard to create.

You need, therefore, authoritative ushers who are able to enforce the rules requiring tardy audience members to wait until the end of a piece to enter the hall. This can be quite a difficult task, as the concertgoers with the potential for causing the most disruption—those sitting down front— are often the ones who have paid the most for their tickets or who are patrons of the concert. It is not a job for young people, those who are timid, or those who can easily be manipulated.

Ask the ushers not to wait until you are about to begin, but to prohibit entrance to the hall as soon as the stage lights come up so that your entire entrance will be free from distraction. In a large hall, it is preferable for the head usher and the stage manager to be in communication with one another so they may coordinate the moment of your entrance in this way.

GET TO KNOW YOUR HELPERS

Performers will get the best support from staff with whom they have established clear and respectful communication. This communication should be carried out early enough so that the staff, in turn, can also plan, as it is sometimes difficult or impossible for them to accommodate last minute requests.

Go to the trouble of remembering the names of your helpers and knowing their various responsibilities. This familiarity will facilitate your interaction. Draw on their expertise. They are essential to the smooth running of your performance.

Chapter 11

Auditions and Competitions

There are no auditions, only performances.

—Janet Bookspan (contemporary), performance coach/stage director

There is a body of literature in the fields of psychology and education confirming that your physical appearance affects the expectations people have of your eventual performance in any area. Performers with good visual attributes are consistently rated higher than others. Studies have also confirmed, though, that the musician's physical appearance has less to do with the conventional standard of attractiveness than with the portrayal of confidence and good stage manners.

Whether they are aware of it or not, judges in a musical audition form an opinion of you before you play, and their evaluation of your appearance and demeanor onstage is included in their evaluation of your playing. They will be responsible for the performances that result from the audition and cannot help but favor performers who not only play well but who also project a poised and confident image. All too often, even in competitions at the highest level, one or more of the best performers is overlooked because of poor stage presence, and prizes are awarded to weaker players who simply look better in front of an audience. For this reason, going into an audition with impeccable stage presence gives you a distinct advantage.

THE AUDITION AS A PERFORMANCE

An audition is no different from any other performance, except that there is usually a specific goal: you may or may not be accepted to a conservatory, secure a position in a performing ensemble, win a prize, or get a teaching post based on the results of an audition. A single audition could thus have a profound effect on your life, and there is no aspect of stage presence that is unimportant in this context. Never decide ahead of time, because you do not expect to win or because the outcome is not that important to you, that your presentation is unimportant.

Typically, you will be performing in an unfamiliar venue. Therefore, you would be smart to anticipate your every possible need and to be as self-sufficient as possible, saving yourself the stress of having to deal with emergency situations without being prepared.

LIST 11.1   THINGS TO BRING TO THE AUDITION OR COMPETITION: CHECKLIST FOR PERFORMERS

- Directions to the event
- Instructions for the event
- Important phone numbers (teachers, page turner, event director)
- Cell phone (with ringer turned off), or change or phone card for phone calls
- Pencil, pen, and paper
- Instrument, cleaned and polished
- Required equipment (adjustable chair, footrest, pedal extender, endpin, mute, music stand, clips for printed music)
- Instrument cleaning and repair supplies
- Scores for judges (*not* your working copy)
- Metronome with a light-only feature
- Wristwatch (but do not wear it when performing)
- Performing attire: clothes, shoes, and accessories
- Wool gloves and jacket or sweater
- Grooming needs: comb, hairbrush, tissues, makeup, nail clipper
- Handkerchief, clean, folded, and pressed
- Eyeglasses (even if you wear contacts)
- Bottled water (avoid sugar and caffeine)
- Nutritious snack

Your posture and gait as you walk into a room or onto a stage can project enthusiasm and confidence just as easily as it can project uncertainty and apprehension. Make sure the very first impression you make is a strong and positive one.

If performing on a stage, bowing before you begin will let you collect yourself and draw the other people in the room into your performance, much like at a concert. Attend to all the minute aspects of your bow, because a poor bow will make you look awkward and inexperienced. When performing in a room, a simple smile and hello to the judges may suffice. In either case, do not fail to acknowledge the judges.

If you enter carrying your instrument, do so in a professional and formal manner. Refrain from holding it in a sloppy fashion as you walk and bow, as well as during rests.

Choose your attire as carefully as you would for a concert. Never wear casual clothes for any audition. Wear concert shoes with appropriate hosiery. Fasten your hair well. Wear nothing on fingers and wrists. Keep fingernails short and do not paint them. Never chew gum or hold anything in your mouth.

It is a good idea, no matter what time of year, to bring wool gloves and a jacket or sweater to wear until just before you perform. Public buildings can be uncomfortably cool either from winter weather or air conditioning. Preperformance nerves can also make you feel unnaturally cold. It is important that your hands and body are kept warm as you wait your turn.

When you are in front of judges, eliminate any and all self-conscious mannerisms. Never touch your hair, body, or clothing. Keep your face relaxed in a pleasant expression. Practice not looking either timid or so serious that you look unpleasant or angry. Keep your mouth relaxed. Do not alert the judges to the parts of the program you find difficult by tensing your lips, furrowing your brow, or using any unnecessary gestures or postures. Absolutely never react to mistakes, as this will only draw more attention to them. Remember that the best players make the performance look easy.

Keep your feet and your head still. How you maintain your feet and your head is a reflection of your total state of mind. If you allow your feet or head to fidget, you will appear nervous or frightened. If you beat time with either, your playing will appear labored and not quite ready for performance.

During long rests, remain concentrated and composed. Do not fill the time by fussing with your instrument or performing any unnecessary tasks. Practice standing or sitting comfortably, merely listening with composure and concentration, all the while sustaining good body posture.

If you require an accompanist and/or a page turner for your audition, rehearse your entrance and exit down to the last detail so you will not have to have any conversation in front of the judges. You want to look as if you all know exactly what you are doing.

If you need to use printed music, keep your scores in a ring binder, arranged in the order you will play them. If it is necessary to have any "triptych" or "altarpiece" arrangements of photocopies to avoid page turns, make sure these are opened out before you begin to play. Juggling your instrument and the score can look awkward. Practice doing this beforehand to make the task as smooth as possible. Bear in mind that there may be no surface except the floor on which to put down your instrument. Make any adjustments to the music stand decisively, without fidgeting or spending too much time double-checking its height, tilt, and balance.

Always be prepared for the possibility that the judges may stop you in the middle of a piece and tell you to go to the next one. If the judges stop you, be ready to go on graciously to the next piece. If they stop you in the middle of the last piece on your program, stand and bow as you would have if you had been permitted to finish. Being stopped is not necessarily an indication that the judges do not like your playing. Often it means just the opposite. You may be disappointed that they stop you, especially if it is before you have played what you think is the most impressive section of the music. But regardless of how you may feel about being stopped, look cheerful and think confidently.

Practice ending your program with a look of success on your face as you take your final bow. Walk off with confidence, looking as if you did your best and are happy with yourself and your performance.

INTERACTING WITH JUDGES

You will audition in a room or on a stage. In a room, where you are in close physical proximity to the judges, it is appropriate to say hello to them as you enter. If you hand your scores to the judges yourself, take time to present them graciously, with eye contact and without hurrying. You should never appear as if you are throwing the scores hastily toward them. If performing on a stage with the judges seated in the audience, walk out and bow as if in concert, without saying anything.

Take time to prepare yourself and set the tone of your performance before actually playing the first note. Wait between pieces until the judges tell you to go on unless you have been instructed beforehand to play continuously; in such a case, take time mentally to get ready for each piece on your program as you would in recital.

YOUR SCORES

Do not bring working scores that are extensively marked up to your audition. You do not want the judges to see your teacher's directions or your notes to yourself. If judges have this information before them, it will draw their attention to your potential difficulties. It is almost impossible for them not to lower your grade if you commit an error you were supposed to have corrected in practice.

Figure 11.1.   End the Audition with a Look of Success (Regardless of How You Think You Played).

Use new, pristine scores that are fully intact and clean in appearance. Avoid pedagogical editions, anthologies, or collections geared toward students (these usually have colorful illustrated covers). Rather, use professional editions whenever possible (no pictures). By doing so, you will give the impression that you are a more serious musician even before you begin to play.

Although you want to avoid giving the judges your working copy with personal reminders and annotations, make sure the score you do give them has your notations regarding articulations, ornaments, dynamics, tempo indications, and cuts that reflect exactly how you have prepared the piece. Judges should know that your interpretation, if different from what is printed in the music, is intentional. This is different from having a score marked to draw attention to your problem areas.

Do not use photocopies. Sponsors of auditions and competitions, wanting to adhere strictly to copyright laws, disqualify candidates who appear with illegal copies of their music. If a work is out of print and it is legal to copy it, you may do so, but bring a recent letter from a publisher or retailer to that effect.

Number the measures neatly in the score if they are not already numbered in your edition. One number per line of music to the upper left of the line is best. Judges want to be able to refer to specific places in the music for their comments. Do not write your name on these scores, as the judges are usually not supposed to know who you are.

INTERACTING WITH RIVALS

A competitive musical event is like any competitive sport. There will be winners and there will be losers. Behave graciously both as a winner and as a loser, for you will eventually find yourself in both positions.

Always make it a point to congratulate the winners. If there is a winners' performance at the end of a competition, not only is it courteous to attend, but it is educational as well. Competitors who avoid listening to the other players miss the unique opportunity to observe how others have prepared themselves to participate in the event. Hearing the other participants play is an invaluable experience that will work to your advantage in the next competition.

When you are in the happy position of receiving a prize, always congratulate the other prize winners. Thank the judges and the organizers of the event for giving you the chance to compete. Extend yourself to those around you, and accept congratulations with sincere gratitude.

Judging a musical performance is subjective. Often, at the conclusion of a competition you and others might strongly disagree with the judges' decisions. Feelings can run very high in this situation. You may not only feel personally disappointed by failing to win a prize, but also rightfully angry that you were a victim of poor judging. If you are a winner, you may notice people around you who feel you did not deserve to win.

Discussing and evaluating judges' decisions is an integral part of participating in competitions. There is much to be learned by doing so. Such discussions, however, are never appropriate at the site of the event. No matter how unfair you may think the judging has been, your behavior toward your fellow competitors, the organizers of the event, and even the judges themselves should remain professional, appreciative, and cordial. If you and the people around you are feeling outraged at the results, share these feelings at a later time. Avoid being drawn into conversations critical of the judging, whether in mixed company or off to the side among your own entourage. While in the presence of others, act as if you assume that the judges have done their best and have chosen the most deserving winners, whether you really feel this way or not.

THE BLIND AUDITION

There are situations in which evaluators will hear a candidate from behind a screen, without seeing the player. Most orchestras in the United States and Europe instituted these so-called blind auditions in the late 1970s as a move to overcome the long-standing belief that white men are more competent players than women and minorities. In fact, the percentage of women and minorities in orchestras has indeed risen dramatically since the practice of blind auditions began.

When participating in a blind audition, however, it is important psychologically to take care of your appearance as if the evaluators can see you. You will simply play better when you look good. You may also have contact with members of the hiring organization other than the actual evaluators, and it does not hurt to look as if you are taking the audition seriously in the presence of personnel staff, board members, volunteers, and even stagehands.

THE 100 PERCENT AUDITION

Because the results may have a lasting impact on your life, you want to give judges the most positive impression possible at any audition. When you have gone to the trouble of taking care of the details of your stage presence, judges will immediately understand that you are serious about your work. You will have the added confidence that comes from knowing you look good and are acting appropriately. Often, good stage presence is the only thing that distinguishes winners from losers.

Be generous and sportsmanlike in your dealings with other competitors, organizers, judges, and audience members. Behave appropriately whether you are a winner or a loser, and abide cheerfully by the judges' decisions.

LIST 11.2   WAYS TO KEEP JUDGES
FROM ELIMINATING YOU

- Dress up as for any concert, and pay close attention to all matters of personal grooming.
- Make eye contact with judges on entering the room or hall and greet them with a smile as you hand over your scores. (If the situation is more formal, with you on a stage and the judges sitting in the hall, formally bow to them, making eye contact before and after your bow—before you begin playing—just as you would to any audience.)
- Practice looking and feeling enthusiastic about playing your audition. Make sure this is reflected in all aspects of your body language (posture, walk, facial expression, and so on).
- Provide the judges with scores in good condition, without notes written all over them.
- Bring editions used by professional musicians, not those published for students.
- Refrain from adjusting your hair, eyeglasses, or clothing.
- Eliminate any visible nervous habits.
- Never register displeasure with your performance. Do not react to mistakes through your facial expression or body language.
- When your performance is finished, bow and leave the room or the stage as you would before any audience, with an expression of success and satisfaction on your face.
- Practice your demeanor before judges by acting out the situation.
- Make and study video recordings of yourself.
- Work to improve all details of your presentation.

Chapter 12

How to Teach Stage Presence

Stage presence is a subject that is sorely neglected. . . . It is a critical element in communicating with an audience, and, for that reason it must be taught as part of a student's formal training.

—Anthony LeRoy Glise (contemporary),
guitarist, composer, music editor

Stage presence can be taught and can always be improved. It is not something that most musicians do naturally, even after years of performing in public. Yet, once aware of it, musicians and students alike begin to understand how their overall presentation affects the impression they make, and how they can win over an audience even before they begin to play.

Teachers can provide students with ongoing experience and, over time, give them the ability to look good and feel confident onstage. Some performers—dancers and singers, for example—are generally taught to be more aware of their stage presence than are instrumentalists. In some conservatories, vocal students are required to approach each lesson as a learning experience in their stage presentation, and are required to pay attention to their dress and grooming on lesson days. All music teachers can incorporate the study of stage presence into their teaching.

As with most life skills, the earlier a child is exposed to principles of stage presence the better. These are most effectively taught from the very first music lesson. Do not wait until a student expresses interest in becoming a professional musician. In fact, it is not at all necessary for a music student to eventually end up on a concert stage for these skills to be relevant. Stage presence skills are invaluable in areas other than music. Having the confidence to be comfortable in front of large groups of people and the poise to make a good impression are prerequisites to most kinds of success. If your students emerge from your studio with good stage presence, you will have given them an ability that carries over to all areas of their lives.

DEVELOPING GOOD STAGE PRESENCE IN STUDENTS

Stage presence can be grouped into four components: 1) posture, 2) the bow, 3) dress, and 4) demeanor. Throughout a student's education, from the first lesson to the last, expertise in these four areas can be taught and improved. All four areas require a long time to master. You cannot simply tell students about them and then move on; these are abilities that can be developed only with constant practice and patient reminders over a long period of time.

Posture

Whether learning to play an instrument, sing, or conduct, good posture is an essential part of good technique. Performing music is a physical activity, and good posture keeps the body working naturally and with minimum effort. It is impossible to breathe freely and deeply when the body is not aligned and when the chest cavity is not fully open. Musical performance of any kind requires good, deep breathing and optimum body balance.

Teachers who work with young children have an especially important responsibility for their students' postures, since the physical attitude students adopt at the beginning of music study usually follows them throughout their lives. Those who have attempted to correct poor posture in older students understand this very well.

Whether you teach voice, instruments, or conducting, think of good posture as the first basic element, without which the student will be at a serious disadvantage. Constantly examine, reassess, and work on your own posture. A teacher with poor posture cannot set a good example, and students learn best by example. Cultivate an interest in the science of body balance and alignment and begin to observe the various ways that people stand, sit, and walk. The more you know about this, the more you can help your students. There are a variety of disciplines that help train musicians in posture, balance, and the most effective use of the body: Alexander Technique, tai chi, yoga, and Pilates, to name a few. Becoming an expert to improve your own posture and that of your students requires that you think about it in the case of every student who comes along and every performer you see. As a teacher, it is imperative that you can recognize subtle weaknesses in posture and brief lapses in body balance and that you can suggest ways to correct them.

If you teach an instrument that is played while seated, you will need specialized equipment to teach posture. Make sure you have adjustable seating specific to the instrument you teach, for yourself as well as for the students. With this equipment, you can provide the best example, and you may seat each individual student in a position just right for his or her body, changing the seating as the student's body changes. In some instances, in addition to adjustable chairs, you will need footrests to keep feet from dangling.

Your students will have a variety of bodies, some with naturally better posture than others. Some will have weak lower backs and find it difficult to stand erect or to sit up straight for any length of time. Some will have tight necks and shoulders. Some will find it difficult to hold their heads squarely on top of their spines. Take time at every lesson to adjust your students' posture and require that they play their lesson with an erect yet relaxed body, whether sitting or standing. Teach them, when sitting, to hold their lower back in the same position as it is when they are standing up straight. Elicit the help of parents to check the students' posture during home practice. Do not neglect to teach walking with good posture, so that the students' entrances and exits will look consistent with their bearing as they perform. Assume that a student's posture will probably not improve significantly until you have consistently taught it for many years. Praise a student's good posture, and do not give up on difficult cases. All students can learn to walk and to perform with good posture.

The Bow

In most Western countries, we no longer bow in the course of daily life. Consequently, we have no experience with bowing and no practice doing so. It is no wonder so many performers, from beginners to professionals, seem self-conscious and awkward when they bow, since the only time they do it is on a stage in front of an audience just before they are about to perform.

Make sure that you, the teacher, have practiced your bow until you feel natural and comfortable doing it, and then teach it carefully by having the student practice bowing repeatedly until the action feels natural and comfortable. Teach the several elements of a good bow, beginning with standing with good posture, feet together, arms naturally at the sides, hands relaxed, and looking at the audience with a pleasant facial expression. Then require an unhurried bow, bending at the waist to about 45 degrees from upright, and looking down at the toes, all the while holding the hands in one place at the side and not letting them dangle out in front or

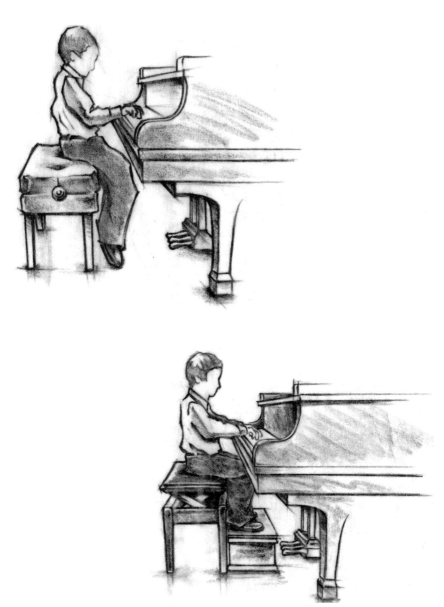

Figure 12.1. Lack of Proper Equipment Results in Poor Posture and Balance; Good Equipment Allows Student to Achieve Strong Posture and Equilibrium.

travel down the legs. The most difficult part of the bow to teach is the end: coming up from the actual bow, standing again with good posture, and reestablishing eye contact with the audience for several moments before moving. This all may seem simple enough, but students will not do it successfully onstage until they have been reminded and have practiced each of these elements over a long period of time.

It helps to give students frequent opportunities to bow in front of small groups. Consistently require good bows in master classes and short recitals as well as in every lesson. Teach students to bow before they play as well as after: bowing at the beginning is the only way they may center themselves and control the timing of their entrances. Take time to evaluate each student's bow. When there is an opportunity, have students critique each other's bows. Make video recordings of performances and observe the video with each individual student for the purpose of evaluating the bows.

It can take years for students to finally feel comfortable enough to perform the bow well, to look poised and self-confident as they face their audience. Be patient, knowing that once this skill is acquired it will stay with them for life.

Dress

When planning recitals for your students, make them formal occasions for which students will want to dress. Distribute a dress code and require strict adherence to it. This may be difficult for students who do not ordinarily have a reason to dress up in their everyday lives or for some who simply hate dressing up. It takes patience and effort to teach the importance of dressing for performances. Explain to students and parents that, just as there are uniforms for various sporting activities, dress clothes are the music student's uniform. Ultimately, your students will respect your enforcement of the dress code, and, though they may complain about it, will come to enjoy the special recital days when they all dress up. Of course, you must set the tone by dressing well, for lessons as well as for performances.

Make everything about your recitals as formal as you can. Have the students perform in a well-maintained hall with a good piano. Place flowers on the stage. Print good-looking programs. Plan a formal reception. Use dressy tablecloths and arrange food attractively on serving platters. Use a punch bowl instead of just setting out soda or juice bottles on a table. These things will add to the overall impression of the recital as a special event that warrants dressing up. As the music teacher, you may need help creating such an elegant reception. Find a parent or a small group of parents who will take on the responsibility, or have the event catered. Of course, not every concert needs to incorporate such an overtly social aspect, but giving students many opportunities to experience performances made special in this way helps them to understand that appropriate demeanor and environment can never be overlooked.

Require that certain aspects of the dress code be observed during lessons. Ask that long hair be fastened back. Instrumentalists should remove everything from fingers (with the possible exception of wedding bands) and wrists, and fingernails must be trimmed. After doing this at lessons year in and year out, students will prepare themselves in this way without even thinking about it.

Impress on students the importance of dressing for *all* performances: recitals, master classes, workshops, auditions, and competitions. Although you may have a less formal dress code for some events, avoid holding any performances for which there are no dress guidelines at all. You do not want to teach students that some concerts are so unimportant that the performers may disregard their presentation. Teach them that looking good in any situation where they will play in front of others will give them an advantage over those who take less care with their appearance.

Regularly critique your students' dress and overall appearance when you review video recordings of their performances with them, making suggestions for improvement. Was the skirt too short? Was the tie straight? Were the shoes too casual? Did the hair fall into the face? Were the clothes too tight? Were the high heels too high? Make the students aware of these issues and remind them, from recital to recital, to think about improving their appearance onstage.

Sample Dress Guidelines for Formal Student Performances

> *Girls:*
> Dressy outfit
> Skirts below the knee (not sheer)
> Sleeves required
> No plunging neckline (or back)
> Fabric should not cling to body
> No stacked shoes or very high heels
> Hosiery required
> *Boys:*
> White or solid dress shirt with a tie
> Dark dress pants (no corduroy or denim) with a dress belt
> Coordinated jacket
> Dress shoes (no sneakers, lug soles, casual suedes)
> Black dress socks

All:
Wear nothing on fingers or wrists
Secure long hair away from the face
Be able to walk naturally in shoes
Clothing and shoes should fit well

Demeanor

If you have taught your students good posture, how to bow, and have required them to dress well, they already feel more confident onstage and in front of an audience. Knowing that you are acting appropriately and looking good contributes to overall poise and self-assurance. You want to further maximize the students' confident appearance by teaching them to eliminate certain gestures or behaviors that might make them look timid, awkward, or nervous, or that may project a bad attitude. Evaluating their performances on video is invaluable in this area.

Facial Expression

Encourage students to maintain a pleasant facial expression as they practice walking and bowing, and also when they play. They can be asked to smile as they bow, but it is important that the smile not look insincere. A sincere and open facial expression, one that conveys a good attitude toward the audience and enthusiasm for the performance, is the goal. The bow at the end should have this same facial expression, whether the student is happy with the performance or not. Teach students never to register displeasure with their performance in any way while onstage. As they perform, teach them not to carry tension in the face, not to grimace, not to look so serious that they appear angry, and not to reveal the most difficult parts of their piece by looking strained when playing them.

In lessons, students should practice not reacting to their own mistakes. Point it out to students whenever they do this, and ask them not to allow themselves to react to their mistakes when they are practicing. Let students know that all performers, even the greatest ones, make mistakes, that there is no such thing as a mistake-free performance. Students will not realize this unless you tell them. Help them understand that all good performers learn to handle mistakes so well that the audience is often unaware of them.

Hands, Feet, and Body

Teach students not to fidget with their hands while onstage. Show them how insecure it looks when performers adjust their clothes or their hair during a concert, and how distracting this can be for their audience. Make sure they know not to scratch an itch or otherwise touch themselves. Tension in hands can be seen from the audience, so teach students how to keep their hands relaxed at all times. This will also have a good effect on their overall ability to stay calm and in control of themselves during a performance.

In lessons, help them learn not to beat time with their feet or head and to eliminate other extraneous body movement.

Attitude

The performer's general attitude is revealed to the audience with the entire body. Every move is a reflection of the player's mental state. Teach students the best pace for walking out onstage and bowing—not sluggish, not hurried. As you work on posture, make sure to include the element of relaxation, because a stiff body projects a nervous or unhappy attitude.

Discuss how to accept compliments at the end of a performance. It is no more appropriate for the performer to register displeasure with his or her performance after the concert than during it. Teach students that it is rude to contradict well-meaning praise—instead, they should accept it graciously and thankfully. Teach them as well never to blame external conditions for a poor performance ("The piano was bad," "Somebody was coughing," "The accompanist threw me off"). Regardless of how poorly a musician feels that he or she may have played, there is no reason to meet the audience afterward without a sense of pride and accomplishment for having performed. Moreover, performers are always much more aware of their own flaws than the audience will be. All students need to realize this.

The best way to teach students to have a good attitude toward their performance is to teach them to love the work they are performing and to love music in general. This, after all, may be the most important job of any music teacher.

ALWAYS TEACH STAGE PRESENCE

Students cannot learn good stage presence if they are asked to exercise it only once or twice a year at a special event. Good stage presence must be an ongoing routine in your studio. Some element of stage presence may be incorporated into every lesson you teach. It takes time and sometimes money to educate musicians in the art of stage presence, but the results are well worth it. As you gradually raise awareness of stage presence among all your students, the standards of your studio will rise accordingly, and the attention you pay to this issue will give students skills that are useful not only in musical performance, but in all other areas of their lives.

Bibliography

Aarons, Martha. "Orchestral Etiquette." *Flute Talk* 17, no. 8 (April 1998): 22.

Alberge, Dalya. "Cover Up, Conductor Tells Fat Fiddlers" (quoting conductor Leonard Slatkin). *London Times,* August 23, 2000.

Baxtresser, Jeanne. "Becoming a Team Player." *Flute Talk* 8, no. 3 (November 1988): 14–17.

Bean, M. "Performance Techniques for Singers: Bringing the Song to Life, part 2: The Two Halves." *Journal of Singing* 54, no. 2 (1997): 39–42.

___. "Performance Techniques for Singers: Gesture in Art Song and Opera." *Journal of Singing* 54, no. 5 (May/June 1998): 37–39.

Beckhelm, Paul. "Take a Bow." *American Music* 7, no. 1 (September/October 1957): 11, 21–22.

Blake, Sara. "Developing a Commanding Stage Presence: A Trained Dancer Looks at the Subject of Musical Performances and Offers Some Eye-Opening Advice." *American Recorder* 39 (May 1998): 16–20+.

Boots, Frederic W. "A Judicious Amount of Showmanship." *Instrumentalist* 25, no. 6 (January 1971): 60–63.

Bryce, Pandora. "Stage Presence and Communication: An Interview with Tenor Mark DuBois." *American Suzuki Journal* 27, no. 4 (Summer 1999): 19–23.

Burns, R. "Showmanship." *Modern Drummer* 11 (September 1987): 110.

Campos, Frank G., ed. "Clinic: Stage Deportment." *ITG Journal* 20, no. 2 (December 1995): 71.

"Capotasto." *Classical Guitar* 5, no. 9 (May 1987): 53.

Cerone, David. "Bringing the Stage into the Practice Room." *American String Teacher* 31, no. 2 (Spring 1981): 24–25.

Clements, Kaye L. "Checklist for Competitions." *Flute Talk* 18, no. 2 (October 1998): 17–22.

Colby, Linda Jenks. "The Rules of Good Page Turning." *Clavier* 28, no. 2 (February 1989): 30.

Collins, Stewart. "Looking Good: There Is More to Concert-Giving Than Going On Stage and Playing the Music." *Classical Music* 654 (March 25, 2000): 46–47.

Davis-Brown, Eileen. "Smile, Please!" *The Strad* 87, no. 1037 (September 1976): 391f.

Debost, M. "Debost's Comments: Limited Movement." *Flute Talk* 17, no. 4 (December 1997): 4–5.

Delano. "Some Tricks of the Trade for Orchestral String Players." *The Strad* 61, no. 725 (September 1950): 156.

Deutsch, R. W. "Slatkin Says Overweight Musicians Should Cover Up." Leonard Slatkin on www.sonicnet.com, 2000.

Duncan, Charles. "Stage Presence." *American String Teacher* 31, no. 2 (Spring 1981): 29.

Ellis, Brobury Pearce. "How Do You Look?" *Music Journal* 9, no. 7 (November 1951): 11, 53–55.

Emmons, Shirlee, and Alma Thomas. *Power Performance for Singers: Transcending the Barriers.* New York: Oxford University Press, 1998.

Fink, Lorraine. "Teaching Stage Personality." *American Suzuki Journal* 27, no. 1 (Fall 1998): 47–48.

Frank, Jonathan. "The Boneless Wonder." *Musical Opinion* 82, no. 976 (January 1959): 233–34.

Gibson, Tom. "Thoughts to Ponder: Auditioning—A View from Behind the Screen." *ITA Journal* 26 (Summer 1998): 20–21.

Glise, Anthony LeRoy. "Stage Presence—the Forgotten Art." *Soundboard* 21, no. 3 (Winter 1995): 21–23.

Goll-Wilson, Kathleen. "Talking about Flutes." *Flute Talk* 15, no. 8 (April 1996): 2.

Gregg, Jean Westerman. "From Song to Speech: On Requirements for a Singing Career." *Journal of Singing* 54 (May/June 1998): 51–52.

Hayes, Susan. "Learning about Showmanship from Opera Stars." *Flute Talk* 15, no. 8 (April 1996): 17–18+.

Hickman, David R. "Judges' Advice to Young Soloists." *ITG Journal* 13, no. 4 (May 1989): 24–25.

Highstein, Ellen. *Making Music in Looking Glass Land: A Guide to Survival and Business Skills for the Classical Performer.* New York: Concert Artists Guild, 1997.

Hill, Paul. "Cleaning Up Your Act: The Pride of Presentation Affects the Pride of Performance." *Choral Journal* 19, no 8 (April 1979): 18–21.

Jacobson, Joshua R. "Before the Concert." *Choral Journal* 21, no. 7 (March 1981): 37+.

Jarboe, John C. "The Last Word: Smile." *American Suzuki Journal* 21, no. 2 (February 1993): 46–47.

Landy, D., and H. Sigall. "Beauty Is Talent: Task Evaluations as a Function of the Performer's Physical Attractiveness." *Journal of Personality and Social Psychology* 29, no. 3 (March 1974): 299–304.

"A Lesson in Concert Etiquette." *School Music* (January/February 1936): 7.

McClaren, Cort Alan. "The Influence of Visual Attributes of Solo Marimbists on Perceived Qualitative Response of Listeners." Ph.D. diss., University of Oklahoma, 1985.

____. "The Visual Aspect of Solo Marimba Performance." *Percussive Notes* 27, no. 1 (Fall 1988): 54–58.

Miller, Richard. "Self-Perception and Performance Reality." *NATS Bulletin* 48, no. 2 (November/December 1991): 14+.

Monroe, Ervin. "Musical Birds." *Flute Talk* 13, no. 1 (September 1993): 27–29.

Morrison, Richard. "So What Is the Bottom Line, Mr. Blobby?" *London Times*, August 23, 2000.

Muegel, Glenn Allen. "Accepting Applause Is Part of the Performance." *National School Orchestra Association Bulletin* 23, no. 2 (January 1981): 11.

Novotna, Jarmila. "What to Do on the Stage?" *Etude* 70 (September 1952): 9, 56–57.

Rathbone, Basil. "How Do You Look to Your Audience?" *Etude* 69 (March 1951): 16, 56.

Scharnberg, William. "Lookin' Good but Feelin' Bad." *The Horn Call* 26, no. 2 (1996): 45–46.

Smythe, Richard. "Mirror Image." *Music Teacher* 76 (September 1997): 15.

Sorel, Claudette. *Mind Your Musical Manners . . . Off and On Stage: A Handbook of Stage Etiquette Plus . . . a Listing of the Important Domestic and Foreign Competitions.* New York: Edward B. Marks, 1972.

____. *Mind Your Musical Manners . . . On and Off Stage: A Handbook of Stage Etiquette,* 3rd ed. New York: Edward B. Marks/Hal Leonard, 1995.

Spelman, Leslie P. "Neglected Aspects of Music Teaching." *American Music Teacher* 17, no. 4 (February/March 1968): 35+.

Street, George Hotchkiss. "Performance Hints for the Young Singer." *Music of the West* 10, no. 9 (May 1955): 5.

Thatcher, E. C. "Mannerisms." *The Strad* 59, no. 708 (April 1949): 304.

Van Ingen, Elizabeth. "Stage Smarts: Concert Etiquette for Performers." *Chamber Music* 2, no. 4 (Winter 1985): 25–27, 46.

Verdery, B. "Contemporary Classical: Performance Tips." *Guitar Player* 24, no. 5 (May 1990): 116.

Vorreiter, Vicki. "To Bow or Not to Bow? . . . That Is the Question!" *American Suzuki Journal* 23, no. 2 (February 1995): 46–47.

Wapnik, Joel, Jolan Kovacs Mazza, and Alice-Ann Darrow. "Effects of Performer Attractiveness, Stage Behavior, and Dress on Violin Performance Evaluation." *Journal of Research in Music Education* 46, no. 4 (Winter 1998): 510–21.

Whitlock, Weldon. *Facets of the Singer's Art.* Vol. 1, *Twentieth Century Masterworks on Singing.* Champaign, Ill.: Pro Musica, 1967.

____. "Stage Deportment." *NATS Bulletin* 21, no. 2 (December 1964): 20–21, 31–32.

Index

About the Author

Karen A. Hagberg, Ph.D., is a consultant and presenter on stage presence for performing musicians. As one of only a dozen Americans to earn a diploma in piano at the Talent Education Institute in Japan, she has traveled widely, conducting seminars and workshops for piano teachers in Australia, Singapore, England, Canada, and throughout the United States since 1990. Her students perform regularly at national and international events and have won several prizes in competitions.

A contributor to the latest editions of *Grove's Dictionary of Opera* and *Grove's Dictionary of Music and Musicians*, Dr. Hagberg has also written numerous articles as author of her personal monthly newsletter while studying in Japan (*Matsumoto News*, 1989–1991), and as editor of the bimonthly *Piano Basics Foundation News* since 1995.

Dr. Hagberg is a graduate of Syracuse University and received her M.A. and Ph.D. degrees at the Eastman School of Music. The writing of this book was motivated by her passion for live, acoustic musical performance and her fervent hope that it will flourish and endure into the twenty-first century and beyond.